FINNEY
ON REVIVAL

Books by
Charles G. Finney
FROM BETHANY HOUSE PUBLISHERS

Autobiography of Charles G. Finney[1]
Believer's Secret of Spiritual Power[2]
Finney on Revival[3]
Finney's Systematic Theology
Lectures on Revival
Principles of Liberty[4]
Principles of Prayer[4]
Principles of Revival[4]
Principles of Sanctification[4]
Principles of Union With Christ[4]
Principles of Victory[4]

[1]Condensed and edited by Helen Wessel   [2]With Andrew Murray
[3]Condensed and edited by V. Raymond Edman   [4]Compiled and edited by Louis G. Parkhurst, Jr.

FINNEY
ON REVIVAL

V. RAYMOND EDMAN

BETHANYHOUSE
PUBLISHERS
MINNEAPOLIS, MINNESOTA

Finney on Revival
Copyright © 2000
Bethany House Publishers

Originally published as *Finney Lives On*. © 1951 Scripture Press
Foundation. First Bethany House edition of *Finney Lives On*, 1971.

Edited and updated by Nancy Renich

Cover by Eric Walljasper

Published by Bethany House Publishers
A Ministry of Bethany Fellowship International
11400 Hampshire Avenue South, Bloomington, Minnesota 55438
www.bethanyhouse.com

Printed in the United States of America by
Bethany Press International, Bloomington, Minnesota 55438

Library of Congress Cataloging-in-Publication Data

Edman, V. Raymond (Victor Raymond), 1900–1967.
    Finney on revival: a study of Charles Finney's revival methods and
message by / V. Raymond Edman. — Updated ed. / revised and updated by
Nancy Renich.
        p. cm.
    1. Revivals. 2. Finney, Charles Grandison, 1792–1875. I. Renich,
Nancy. II. Title.
BV3790 .E293   2000
269'.2—dc21   00–010799

To the faithful sons and daughters of Wheaton College,
who sat with me night and day in God's presence
when the Spirit of God brought refreshing from heaven,
reviving our hearts and regenerating the lost.
Life will never be the same again for the hearts
who have known the personal workings of the Holy Spirit
in their own lives.

Acknowledgments

I am deeply grateful to Rowena P. Carr and Deborah Kallberg Wade of the president's office at Wheaton College for their gracious and efficient help in the preparation of this manuscript. I am also thankful to the librarians who were tireless in finding source materials for me so that the message on revival might be made available to all.

These co-workers were with the college family in the days and nights of heart-searching and cleansing that came to the campus of Wheaton College by the sweet reviving of God's Spirit in early 1950.

Preface

This volume on Finney is written and compiled from a deep burden and burning heart for true revival, for refreshing from on high, for the "days of heaven upon earth" of which we read in the experience of God's people in past times.

In all of my reading on revival, I have found nothing equal to Finney's *Lectures on Revival*, which I have here attempted to condense for the modern reader. They constitute lessons that God's servant learned in the days when tens of thousands came to a saving knowledge of the Lord Jesus. I have found nothing more heart-searching, more pungent and powerful, or more satisfying than these messages by Charles G. Finney.

The lectures in their original form were quite long and detailed, with a lot of dated material and references to personalities and controversies long since forgotten. Therefore, it occurred to me that a condensation should be made that would preserve the substance of Finney's teaching in his own words. Added to the lectures is a biographical study of Finney, so that we have the evangelist and his message in their historical setting and also some of his messages in condensed form.

This book is published with the earnest prayer that it be read diligently and its principles be followed implicitly, and that there be revival in our time.

V. Raymond Edman
Wheaton College, 1951
Wheaton, Illinois

Contents

Publisher's Note

In an effort to reach the reader of the twenty-first century with Finney's timeless message, we have opted to further condense and revise this excellent work by V. Raymond Edman.

Finney preached, lectured, and wrote to a decidedly different audience, but his message, inspired by the Holy Spirit, is applicable to God's people today.

Foreword

I once took an entire summer to soak my soul in the writings of Charles G. Finney. What it did for me, and the changes it made in my ministry, will never be forgotten.

Charles Finney was nothing if not sincere; he was desperately in earnest. Everything about his preaching proclaims the fact that if you don't intend to mean business with God, you'd better stop listening altogether and go home—or words to that effect. As a matter of fact, he sometimes dismissed congregations that he thought were too apathetic and indifferent—thus serving the dual purpose of angering them enough to make them think and deeply convicting them of their need.

One of the key words of Finney's life and ministry was *urgency*. This became evident soon after his conversion. He began to spend considerable time among the people of the community, witnessing to them of their need of Christ. His own elderly father burst into tears when Finney said in response to his greeting, "I am well, Father, body and soul. But, Father, you are an old man; all your children are grown up and have left your house; and I have never heard a prayer in [your] house." It was not long after this that the elder Finney was gloriously converted.

What was true of these first days of Finney's Christian experience was seen throughout his life. He always prayed and preached with such conviction as to convince his hearers of the extreme and eternal importance of his words.

The Word of God took first place in Finney's thinking and sermon preparation. He said on one occasion, "I read nothing all that winter but my Bible." He was consistently in the Word of God so that his messages had the force of the flaming sword. Finney was also faithfully among the people to witness to them of God's saving grace and their need of the risen Christ in their lives. If it is true that Finney spent many hours in private prayer—usually before daybreak—it is also true that many of his other non-preaching hours were spent among the people of the community, dealing with them regarding their souls. This, of course, made his preaching immensely practical and, on occasion, embarrassingly pointed.

Finney always related his sermons to everyday life. Sermon building went on as he walked through the community and observed people in any number of situations. These illustrations he would deftly work into his preaching. His messages had a kind of pile driver effect: they drove away at a point until it was firmly established in his hearers' thinking.

Finney believed that preaching should result in some kind of decision or resolution—that is, immediate action and not simply contemplation. He made abundantly clear that you may do whatever you wish concerning the message of God—accept it or reject it—but you will have to decide something.

The greatness of this man was enhanced by his humanity. He was never too high in the theological clouds to come down to the practical business of living. He believed that revival in the sense of a real stirring among God's people was based squarely upon certain unchanging principles, and he was far too much of a realist to suppose that any amount of fancy religious talk or praying could take the place of ruthless honesty and sacrificial obedience.

We could use a few of his kind today!

Dr. Edman's study of the life of Finney came for him as it did for me, out of a great hunger of heart for revival. If there is one thing his leadership has meant to the students of Wheaton College—and to the evangelical world at large—it is his constant yearning toward an Almighty God and continual Spirit-led obedience to His commands—a process that takes many others along the way to revival.

Dr. Edman has captured the atmosphere that surrounded the ministry of Finney and has woven his own charming style into a highly readable and exceedingly profitable book. May it be to his readers as it has been to me—a source of great conviction and inspiration.

Robert A. Cook

Come, Holy Spirit, come!
    Let Thy bright beams arise;
Dispel the darkness from our minds,
    And open all our eyes.

Revive our drooping faith,
    Our doubts and fears remove,
And kindle in our breast the flame
    Of never-dying love.

Convince us of our sin;
    Then lead to Jesus' blood;
And to our wondering view reveal
    The secret love of God.

'Tis Thine to cleanse the heart,
    To sanctify the soul,
To pour fresh life on every part,
    And new create the whole.

Dwell therefore in our hearts;
    Our minds from bondage free;
Then shall we know, and praise, and love
    The Father, Son, and Thee.

A Background of the Times

In the early autumn of 1825, the canal boat *Seneca Chief*, colorfully decorated and bearing a distinguished party on board—the guests of Governor DeWitt Clinton—moved steadily through the new Erie Canal across New York State, from the young and blustering port of Buffalo to the more austere and settled Albany on the Hudson River, and then down that noble stream to the sea. On the arrival of the *Seneca Chief* at the port of New York, the governor, with appropriate ceremony, poured a keg of Lake Erie water into the Atlantic to symbolize the newly established union between the Great Lakes of North America and the Seven Seas of the world. At long last the Erie Canal had become a reality, and because of it the wilderness of central New York State would soon be transformed into flourishing villages and farms, and a new epoch in American expansion toward the setting sun would be under way.

The Erie Canal constitutes a very apt symbol of the ministry of Charles G. Finney, who, in my opinion, was America's most widely known and successful revivalist. His early ministry was largely in the area along the banks of the Canal, and frequently he used the slow but steady means of transportation made available by it. Like the Canal, he was a channel of blessing and usefulness, transforming the wilderness of American hearts. The rough places were made plain, the crooked was made straight, farmers and woodsmen, merchants and lawyers were converted, all because a Spirit-filled man brought the dynamic gospel of Christ to the new villages and cities along the Canal as well as eastward into New England and westward into the Ohio country.

Just as a larger and better America was made possible, socially and economically, by the Erie Canal, just so a new America in the spiritual sense was made by the ministry of Charles Finney. Just as the Canal was a channel for American commerce and enterprise, so Finney's life was a channel for the river of God to bring saving grace, morality, integrity, sobriety, and godliness to American life.

The significance of Finney's contribution to the spiritual life of America stands out clearly as one views the historical setting of his ministry. Before his day there had come two mighty visitations of God's Spirit to America, known as the First and Second Awakenings. The first came in the 1740s to the Colonies during the days of Jonathan Edwards, Gilbert Tennent, George Whitefield, and others, and revival had strengthened and steeled Colonial hearts for the fiery ordeal of the long French and Indian Wars on the frontier and the Revolution for American freedom. The Second Awakening came at the turn of the nineteenth century when the young republic was beginning to feel its internal strength and external independence.

In the day when principles of the new constitution were beginning to be applied to American life, and western expansion began to turn American eyes from European conflicts and ambitions, the spiritual life of America was threatened by the impact of English deism and French infidelity. Voltaire and Thomas Paine were the heroes of American schoolboys, who called each other by French names, as was done in the Revolution against the Bourbons. Orthodoxy was not coping well with the insidious and insistent infidelity that had crept into the church. And then revival came to America—first to New England through the ministry of Timothy Dwight, President of Yale, and then to the new west of Kentucky and Tennessee through a host of Methodist circuit riders and Baptist preachers. Within a decade of the Second Awakening, all of American life had been lifted to new spiritual and moral heights.

Finney's half century of revival ministry brought the dynamic of the gospel to a very needy nation. The impact of the Second Awakening had decreased markedly by the time Finney appeared in the rural areas of central New York in the third decade of the nineteenth century. Strident voices were heard in the land and strife seemed always imminent. American expansionism, not satisfied by the acquisition of the Louisiana Territory and Florida, was reaching westward to Texas, California, and Oregon. By the Monroe Doctrine, Americans had declared the Western Hemisphere to be an area of particular interest and apart from the power politics of Europe. Strong men with strong opinions stood in high places in American political life—Andrew Jackson, Henry Clay, Daniel Webster, and John C. Calhoun.

Sectional strife was on the increase, with bitterness between the North and South over the tariff and the nullification position of South Carolina, over the domination of American economic life by the United States Bank, and especially over the slavery issue. The Missouri Compromise of 1820 had called to action the aging Jefferson and his contemporaries like a fire alarm in the night. The Compromise did not quell the fire on the frontier. William Lloyd Garrison, Wendell Phillips, and other abolitionists continued to stir the Northern conscience and to anger Southern conviction. The Wilmot Proviso greatly complicated and embittered the acquisition of Texas and territories gained in the Mexican War, and the conflagration was not quenched by the

Compromise of 1850. The Kansas-Nebraska Act of 1854 and the Dred Scott Decision of 1857 raised the issue of slavery in the territories to a fevered pitch. The "Freeport Doctrine" of Senator Douglas, flouting the Dred Scott Decision in his debates with Lincoln, split irretrievably the Democratic Party and made possible the election of Lincoln to the presidency in 1860. The days of impending crisis, with their venality of partisan politics and vindictiveness of sectional strife, to which one must add the vulgarity of the frontier and the vice of growing cities, called loudly and imperatively for a prophet of God.

Finney emerged like John the Baptist from the wilderness to prepare the way of the Lord and to preach with the fire of the Holy Spirit the urgency of repentance, sparing neither the sophisticated Pharisees in smug, respectable religion nor the insatiable publicans in greedy, grafting politics. Finney was God's man for that day of strife and sinfulness.

————————

The purpose of this volume is to reevaluate the principles and teachings of Finney and to show that though they are from a different age and different worldview, they are decidedly applicable to modern America. Finney knew the secret of revival and its strength. For the past several years there has come to me and to many others a deep burden for the return of revival in America. I have read and reread Finney's *Autobiography* and his *Revival Lectures*[1] and have come to the persuasion that to a large extent we do not see revival because we do not know its pattern or the mighty moving of God's Spirit as Finney did. There are few books as packed with spiritual power as these.

"LORD, I have heard of your fame; I stand in awe of your deeds, O LORD. Renew them in our day, in our time make them known; in wrath remember mercy" (Habakkuk 3:2).

---

[1] A condensed version of his autobiography is available through Bethany House. *Revival Lectures*, published in 1868 by Revell, is out of print. See Sources and Recommended Reading at the back of this book.

Lord, I hear of showers of blessing
Thou art scattering full and free,
Showers the thirsty land refreshing;
Let some portion fall on me.

Pass me not, O tender Savior,
Let me love and cling to Thee;
I am longing for Thy favor;
Whilst Thou art calling, O call me!

Pass me not, O mighty Spirit,
Thou canst make the blind to see;
Witnesser of Jesus' merit,
Speak the word of power to me!

Love of God, so pure and changeless,
Blood of Christ, so rich and free,
Grace of God, so strong and boundless,
Magnify them all in me, even me!

PART ONE

The Man

1

The Penitent Prays

Finney lives on!

He was very much alive during his long career of eighty-four years, and his twilight years found him still mentally alert and spiritually vigorous. Most of the pictures in common circulation of the great evangelist portray an elderly man, his appearance made even older than his advanced years by the full beard that was the pride of American gentlemen in the middle nineteenth century. In my opinion, we should remember him as he was in the days of his strength—during the tireless thirties, the fearless forties, and the furious fifties, when he was the fiery prophet of revival in American backwoods settlements and seaboard cities, and beyond the seas to Britain.

As a lad he was a typical American boy, accustomed to the arduous labor of the pioneer farm. He was rugged and athletic, a child of the woodland and also of the waters. Of Finney it was said, "When he was twenty, he excelled every man and boy he met in every species of toil or sport. No man could throw him, no man could knock his hat off, no man could run faster, jump farther,

leap higher, or throw a ball with greater force and precision"
[source unknown].

He was an expert marksman, and long past middle life he still
enjoyed hunting wild game in field and forest. He grew to a height
of six feet, two inches. The knowledge of seamanship gained
aboard small sailing boats on Lake Ontario stood him in good
stead in later life, especially on a trip to the Mediterranean in a
small brig when he had to take the place of an inebriated skipper.

His father, Sylvester Finney, was a farmer and a veteran of the
Revolutionary War. Charles was born on August 29, 1792, in Warren, Connecticut. While not a frontiersman, he was born into the
generation of pioneer New England farmers who turned their
faces from the more settled areas of the land to venture into the
relatively unbroken wilderness of middle New York State.

In oxcarts and covered wagons, the soldiers of the Revolution
and their families moved across the Hudson to fields yet uncon-
quered, and with them went the Finney family to Oneida County
in New York when Charles was two years of age. True to the custom of the time, the family moved often—first to Kirkland, and
later to the shores of Lake Ontario near Sackett's Harbor. Finney
was heir of the spirit and tradition of the frontier that molded
strong Americans in days that were rugged and rough. In him one
sees the trace of independence, self-reliance, optimism, strong
convictions, ingenuity, nonconformity to accepted and artificial
standards, and a consciousness of American destiny that were
characteristic of the frontier. He was thoroughly democratic in his
outlook on life, with confidence in the judgment of the people to
determine their own affairs; and when he was converted, he
maintained vigorously that government should be conducted in
the fear of God.

His education in the local log schoolhouses and in Hamilton
Oneida Institute was only partial at best, and yet he took the
greatest possible advantage of his opportunities. For some years
he taught in country schools in Connecticut and New Jersey,
which proved to be an excellent regimen for later service as a

teacher of the Word. He was dissuaded from attending Yale, even though he was already a good classical scholar in his own right, on the ground that he could achieve the substance of college training on his own initiative. He loved music and invested his early earnings in a cello on which he excelled.

By twenty-six he had determined to follow the legal profession, so in 1818 he entered the law office of Judge Benjamin Wright in Adams, New York, as an apprentice. With customary zeal Finney applied himself wholeheartedly to his studies as well as to the social life of the community, and after a period of two years was admitted to the bar and became a member of the judge's law firm. Law was a profession of unusual possibilities in the early decades of the American republic. The nation was growing westward, commerce and industry were multiplied, farmers had both good years and bad, and a lawyer had the opportunity to hitch his kite to the rising star of American destiny. Finney was an active lawyer and a good one.

Until he was twenty-nine, the schoolteacher and lawyer had paid very little attention to religious matters. His parents had not concerned themselves with the gospel or given much religious training, if any, to their children. On occasion, Finney attended church services, but found the sermons to be dull and uninteresting, even boring, and those he heard while teaching school in New Jersey were given in German. Of himself, Finney had to say, *"When I went to Adams to study law I was almost as ignorant of religion as a heathen. I had been brought up mostly in the woods. I had very little regard to the Sabbath and had no definite knowledge of religious truth."*

In Adams, he came for the first time under the preaching of an educated minister, the Reverend George W. Gale, a Princeton graduate. The young pastor and the young lawyer became fast friends, even though they did not understand each other. Gale was a disciple of the "old school," with a theological position that could be described as "hyper-Calvinistic." Finney knew nothing as yet of systematic theology. In his study of law he had come across many biblical quotations, especially from the Mosaic Code, with the result that he purchased a Bible for himself and had begun to read it with interest but with little understanding. The conversations between preacher and lawyer left the latter more mystified than enlightened.

To a man of Finney's mental acumen, it seemed that many questions were left unanswered and many terms undefined. In reviewing that part of his life, Finney wrote,

> What did he mean by repentance? Was it a mere feeling of sorrow for sin? Was it altogether a passive state of mind or did it involve a voluntary element? If it was a change of mind, in what respect was it a change of mind? What did he mean by the term *regeneration*? What did such language mean when applied to a spiritual change? What did he mean by faith? Was it merely an intellectual state? Was it merely a conviction or persuasion that the things stated in the gospel were true?

The lawyer's questions remained unanswered and his perplexity deepened by the apparent inconsistency between the prayers of Christians and the lack of answers to their prayers. To him it seemed that they prayed without expecting an answer, despite the promises to be found in the Scriptures. They prayed for a revival of religion, for instance, but nothing happened. With characteristic discernment, he commented to some of his neighbors, *"You have prayed enough since I have attended these meetings to have prayed the devil out of [town], if there is any virtue in your prayers. But here you are praying on, and complaining still."* Finney was later to learn that many questions are not settled by definition of terms or deftness of argument, but only by coming to know personally the Lord Jesus Christ, in whom are hidden all the treasures of wisdom and knowledge. Then he understood that "the fear of the Lord is the beginning of wisdom."

Nevertheless, his experience should warn us that there may be many honest seekers who do not find the true way because their problems and perplexities are not squarely addressed by their

Christian friends and acquaintances. Dogma without definition of terms can bring deadness of spirit, theology without thought can bring confusion, and Scripture without the searchlight of the Spirit can be the savor of death unto death. The thoughtful unbeliever is bewildered rather than awakened by our religious vernacular understood only by the church.

Despite the mental difficulties that could not be dissipated by the preacher or his parishioners, Finney did come to the persuasion that the Bible was the true Word of God. *"This being settled,"* he added, *"I was brought face-to-face with the question of whether I would accept Christ as presented in the gospel or pursue a worldly course of life. At this period, my mind, as I have since known, was much impressed by the Holy Spirit, so that I could not long leave this question; nor could I long hesitate between the two courses of life presented to me."*

The story of Finney's conversion is in many respects like that of Saul of Tarsus. To be sure, Finney, unlike the student of Gamaliel, was not instructed in religion, nor did he oppose the gospel, but both were mature men who were energetic, intelligent, inquisitive, dynamic, and of strong convictions. And in both cases conversion was radical, a complete about-face from their previous way of life. It seems both came face-to-face with the Savior, and then, broken in human pride and self-reliance, went from their soul-transforming experience of Christ to become winners of souls. Finney, like the great apostle, was not at first entirely accepted among his own, and seems to have spent a year and a half to two years in a wilderness-like experience, and in weeks and months of stillness he learned the gospel from the Scriptures.

On many occasions the apostle Paul told with great feeling his experience of meeting the Savior at the Gate of Damascus, and in like manner Finney never lost the glow of the day and the hour when he came to a saving knowledge of the Lord Jesus. Here is his own story (somewhat condensed and revised), a classic in itself:

On a Sabbath evening in the autumn of 1821, I made up

my mind that I would settle the question of my soul's salvation at once, that if it were possible I would make my peace with God. But as I was very busy in the affairs of the office, I knew that without great firmness of purpose, I should never effectually attend to the subject. I therefore then and there resolved, as far as possible, to avoid all business, and everything that would divert my attention, and to give myself wholly to the work of securing the salvation of my soul. I carried this resolution into execution as sternly and thoroughly as I could. I was, however, obliged to be a good deal in my office. But as the providence of God would have it, I was not much occupied either on Monday or Tuesday, and had opportunity to read my Bible and engage in prayer most of the time.

Conviction increased, but still it seemed as if my heart grew harder. I could not shed a tear; I could not pray. In fact, I had no opportunity to pray aloud, and frequently I felt that if I could be alone where I could use my voice and let myself go, I should find relief in prayer.

Tuesday evening I became very nervous and in the night a strange feeling came over me as if I were about to die. I knew that if I did I would sink down to hell, but I quieted myself as best I could until morning.

At an early hour I started for the office, but just before I arrived, something seemed to confront me with questions like *"What are you waiting for? Did you not promise to give your heart to God? What are you trying to do? Are you endeavoring to work out a righteousness of your own?"*

At this point, the whole question of gospel salvation opened to my mind in a manner most marvelous to me. I think I then saw, as clearly as I ever have in my life, the reality and fullness of the atonement of Christ. I saw that His work was a finished work, and that instead of having or needing any righteousness of my own to recommend me to God, I had to submit myself to the righteousness of God through Christ. Gospel salvation seemed to me to be an offer of something to be accepted, and that it was full and complete. All that was necessary on my part was to consent to give up my sins and accept Christ. Salvation, it seemed to me, instead of being something to be accomplished by my own works, was something to be found entirely in the Lord Jesus Christ, who presented himself before me as my God and my Savior.

Without my being distinctly aware of it, I had stopped in the street right where the inward voice seemed to arrest me. How long I remained in that position, I cannot say. But after this distinct revelation had fixed itself in my mind, the question seemed to be put, *"Will you accept it now, today?"* I replied, *"Yes; I will accept it today, or I will die in the attempt."*

North of the village and over a hill, stood a stretch of woods, in which I was in the almost daily habit of walking when the weather was pleasant. It was now October, and the time was past for my frequent walks there. Nevertheless, instead of going to the office, I turned and bent my course toward the woods, feeling that I must be alone, and away from all human eyes and ears, so that I could pour out my prayer to God.

But when I attempted to pray, I found that my heart would not pray. I had supposed that if I could only be where I could speak aloud, without being overheard, I could pray freely. But when I came to try, I was dumb, that is, I had nothing to say to God; or at least I could say but a few words, and those without heart. In attempting to pray, I would hear a rustling in the leaves and would stop and look up to see if somebody were coming. This I did several times.

Finally I found myself fast on the verge of despair. I said, *"I cannot pray. My heart is dead to God, and will not pray."* I then reproached myself for having promised to give my heart to God before I left the woods. When I came to try, I found I could not do it. My inward soul hung back and there was no reaching out to God. I began to feel deeply that it was too late, that it must be that God had given up on me and I was past hope.

I thought about the rashness of my promise that I would give my heart to God that day or die in the attempt. It seemed to me that it was binding upon my soul and yet I was going to break my vow. A great discouragement came over me and I felt almost too weak to remain on my knees.

Just at this moment I again thought I heard someone approach and opened my eyes to see whether it were so. But right there the revelation of my pride of heart as the great difficulty that stood in the way was distinctly shown me. An overwhelming sense of my wickedness at being ashamed to have a human being see me on my knees before God took such powerful possession of me that I cried at the top of my voice and exclaimed that I would not leave that place if all the men on earth and all the devils in hell surrounded me. *"What!"* I said, *"such a degraded sinner as I am, on my knees confessing my sins to the great and holy God, and ashamed to have any human being, a sinner like myself, find me on my knees endeavoring to make my peace with my offended God!"* The sin appeared awful to me and it broke me down before the Lord.

Just at that point this passage of Scripture seemed to drop into my mind with a flood of light: *"Then shall ye go and pray unto me, and I will hearken unto you. Then shall ye seek me and find me, when ye shall search for me with all your heart."* I instantly seized hold of this with my heart. I had intellectually believed the Bible before, but never had the truth been in my mind that faith was a voluntary trust instead of an intellectual state. I was as conscious as I was of my existence of trusting at that moment in God's veracity. Somehow I knew that it was a passage of Scripture, though I do not think I had ever read it. I knew that it was God's Word and God's voice that spoke to me. I cried to Him, *"Lord, I take thee at thy Word. Now thou knowest that I do search for thee with all my heart, and that I have come here to pray to thee; and thou hast promised to hear me."*

That seemed to settle the question that I could that day perform my vow. The Spirit seemed to lay stress upon that idea in the text, "When you search for me with all your heart . . ." The question of when seemed to fall heavily on my heart. I told the Lord that I would take Him at his Word, that He could not lie, and that I was sure He heard my prayer and that He would be found of me.

I went to dinner and found I had no appetite to eat. I then went to the office and found that my colleague had gone to dinner. I took down my cello and, as I was accustomed to do, began to play and sing some pieces of sacred music. But as soon as I began to sing those sacred words, I began to weep. It seemed as if my heart were liquid, and my feelings were in such a state that I could not hear my own voice singing without causing my emotions to overflow. I wondered at this, and tried to suppress my tears but could not. I put up my instrument and stopped singing.

After the dinner hour we were engaged in moving our books and furniture to another office. We were very busy at this and had little conversation all afternoon. My mind, however, remained in a profoundly tranquil state. There was a great sweetness and tenderness in my thoughts and feelings. Everything appeared to be going right and nothing seemed to ruffle or disturb me in the least.

Just before evening the thought occurred to me that as soon as I was left alone in the new office I would try to pray again—that I was not going to abandon the subject of religion and give up, and although I no longer had any undue concern about my soul, still I would continue to pray.

By evening we got the books and furniture organized, and I made up a good fire in the open fireplace, hoping to spend the evening alone. Just at dark my colleague, seeing that everything was settled, bade me a good night and went to his home. I had accompanied him to the door, and as I closed it and turned around, my heart seemed to melt again within me. All my feelings seemed to rise and flow out, and the utterance of my heart was, *"I want to pour my whole soul out to God."* The rising of my soul was so great that I rushed into the back room to pray.

There were no fire or light there, but nevertheless it appeared to me as if it were perfectly light. As I went in and shut the door after me, it seemed as if I met the Lord Jesus Christ face-to-face. It did not occur to me then, nor did it for some time afterward, that it was wholly a mental state. On the contrary, it seemed to me that I saw Him as I would see any other man. He said nothing, but looked at me in such a manner as to break me right down at His feet. I have always since regarded this as a most remarkable state of mind, for it seemed to me a reality that He stood before me, and I fell down at His feet and poured out my soul to Him. I wept aloud like a child and made such confessions as I could with my choked utterances. It seemed to me that I bathed His feet with my tears and yet I had no distinct impression that I touched Him.

I must have continued in this state for a good while, but my mind was too absorbed with the encounter to recollect anything that I said. But I know that as soon as my mind became calm enough to break off the interchange, I returned to the front office and found that the fire I had made of large wood was nearly burned out. But as I turned and was about to take a seat by the embers, I received a mighty baptism of the Holy Spirit. Without any expectation of it or ever having a thought in my mind that there was any such thing for me, and without any recollection that I had ever heard of it mentioned by anyone before, the Holy Spirit descended upon me in a manner that seemed to go right through my body and soul like a wave of electricity. Indeed, it seemed to come in waves and waves of liquid love, for I could not express it in any other way. It seemed like the very breath of God. I can recall distinctly that it seemed to fan me like immense wings.

No words can express the wonderful love that was shed abroad in my heart. I wept aloud with joy and love, and literally bellowed out the unutterable fullness of my heart. These waves came over me and over me, one after the other, until I cried out, *"I shall die if these waves continue to pass over me!"* I said, *"Lord, I cannot bear any more"*; yet I had no fear of death.

How long I continued in this state with this baptism continuing to roll over me and through me, I do not know. But I know it was late in the evening when a member of my choir— for I was the director of the choir—came into the office to see me. He found me in this state of loud weeping, and said to me, *"Mr. Finney, what ails you?"* I could give him no answer for some time. He then said, *"Are you in pain?"* I gathered myself together as best I could, and replied, *"No, but so happy that I cannot live."*

At home, I soon fell asleep, but almost as soon awoke again on account of the great flow of the love of God that was in my heart. Then I fell asleep again, and awoke in the same manner. Thus I continued till late into the night, when I obtained some sound repose.

When I awoke in the morning, the sun had risen and was pouring clear light into my bedroom. Words cannot express the impression that it made upon me. Instantly the baptism that I had received the night before returned upon me in the same manner. I arose upon my knees in the bed and wept aloud with joy, and remained for some time too overwhelmed with the baptism of the Spirit to do anything but pour out my soul to God. It seemed as if this morning's baptism was accompanied with a gentle reproof, and the Spirit seemed to say to me, *"Will you doubt? Will you doubt?"* I cried, *"No! I will not doubt; I cannot doubt."* He then cleared up the subject so much in my mind that it was, in fact, impossible for me to doubt that the Spirit of God had taken possession of my soul.

In this state I was taught the doctrine of justification by faith as a present experience. I could now see and understand what was meant by the passage "Being justified by faith, we have peace with God through our Lord Jesus Christ." I could see that in the moment I believed all sense of condemnation had entirely dropped out of my mind, and that from that moment I could not feel a sense of guilt or condemnation by any effort I could make. My sense of guilt was gone; my sins were gone; and I do not think I felt any more sense of guilt than if I had never sinned.

This was just the revelation that I needed. I felt myself justified by faith . . . my heart was so full of love that it overflowed. My cup ran over with blessing and with love . . . I could not recover the least sense of guilt for my past sins. Of this experience I said nothing at the time to anybody.

Charles G. Finney—farmer lad, woodsman, teacher, lawyer—had been led out of uncertainty and heartache into the assurance of sins forgiven, into newness of life in Christ, to become God's child. His experience, perhaps more vivid and dramatic than most, shows the pattern of saving faith: the persuasion that the salvation of his soul was of greater importance than the success of his business; his despair in saving himself; the fear of man that kept him from facing the Savior; the pride that utterly humbled his heart; and the Scriptures that formed the basis for his faith. He was born again of the Word and of the Spirit.

Justified by faith and filled to overflowing with God's Spirit, he was indeed a new creation to whom all things had become new. His boundless energy and ambition were now devoted to the person of the Savior rather than to himself, to service for his Master rather than for self-interest, to the welfare of other souls rather than to amassing wealth for himself. The Law of God was now paramount over the laws of the land, however just and beneficial the latter might be, and he powerfully preached the authority of that Law and the inevitable judgment that follows its breach, until guilty hearts sought the mercy seat of God. The lawyer, redeemed and renewed, went forth to plead at the bar of human hearts, there to present sin in all its grief and degradation, and also to show salvation in its glorious power to change and restore. By the blood of Calvary's cross the blackness of each human heart could be made white as snow, even as he had come to know for himself in that humble hour at the Savior's feet.

2

The Preacher Learns

He who would be a good teacher must himself be teachable and well taught by others. Before entering the legal profession and becoming a Christian, Finney had been a country school-teacher and had learned many lessons in human nature as well as having taught the rudiments of knowledge to his small charges. Throughout his long and effective ministry he was ever a learner of the deep truths of God as well as an expositor of the Scriptures and evangelist extraordinaire. Outstanding among the many lessons he came to learn, all of which are unusually helpful to us, were (1) his knowledge that the dynamic of God's Spirit is available to every believer; (2) that personal and private devotions are indispensable to the development of Christian life; (3) that situations and hearts are changed by prevailing prayer; (4) that obedience to the will of God must be instant and implicit; (5) that effectiveness of service usually spawns envy and opposition in some; and (6) that continued tenderness of heart is the true secret of personal, perennial revival.

Filled With the Spirit

At the very beginning of his Christian life he came to know through firsthand experience the importance of scriptural teachings: "But you will receive power when the Holy Ghost comes on you" (Acts 1:8) and "Be filled with the Spirit" (Ephesians 5:18b). The freshness and the fullness of the divine anointing that he had received was upon him from the very outset of his service. His first few days and weeks as a Christian bear eloquent testimony to the fact that the Spirit-filled Christian is a burning and shining light for the Savior, however dark his generation.

On the day after his conversion, Finney spoke with many of his neighbors and friends and could say, *"I believe the Spirit of God made lasting impressions upon every one of them. I cannot remember one with whom I spoke who was not soon after converted."*

The first person he saw in the law office was his partner, Judge Wright. To Finney's first few words on the subject of salvation, the elder partner looked at Finney with astonishment, dropped his head, and after a few moments left the office under deep conviction. He was not converted until some days later, largely because of pride and the fear of the opinions of others, much as had been the case with Finney. While under conviction, the judge sought to pray in private, even with desperation, but he had determined he would not go into the woods to pray. The day came, however, when from the woods he returned to the law office to say, *"I've got it! I've got it!"* and then to fall on his knees in thanksgiving to God. Finney adds, *"He then gave us an account of what had been passing in his mind and why he had not obtained hope before. He said as soon as he gave up that point and went into the woods, his mind was relieved; and when he knelt down to pray, the Spirit of God came upon him and filled him with unspeakable joy."*

The second person to come into the office on the morning after Finney's conversion was a deacon of the church, who had retained the young lawyer as his attorney for a case to be tried at ten o'clock. To him, Finney made reply, *"I have a retainer from the*

Lord Jesus Christ to plead His cause, and I cannot plead yours," and then added his testimony. The deacon *"dropped his head, and, without making any reply, went out. A few moments later, in passing the window, I observed that he was standing in the road, seemingly lost in deep meditation. He went away, as I afterward learned, and immediately settled his suit."*

Then the newly converted Finney went out into the village streets to talk with others about their soul's salvation. The urgency of the gospel lay heavily upon him. There was no question in his mind as to his call to be a witness for Christ and a preacher of the gospel. The first call was in the shop of a Christian shoemaker, who at that moment was in conversation with a young man defending Universalism. The arguments of the Universalist were immediately demolished by Finney, and without making a reply, the young man went out into the street, over a fence, and into the woods. That evening he returned with a radiant testimony of faith in Christ.

During a visit with other friends later in the day, Finney was asked to say grace at the table. A young man boarding with the family, a professed Universalist, and employed in distilling whisky, rushed from the table, locked himself in his room, and came out in the morning a believer in Christ. He afterward became a minister of the gospel. Without invitation of any kind, the people of Adams made their way to the Presbyterian church that evening, and Finney went with them. Of that service he said, *"No one seemed ready to open the meeting; but the house was packed to capacity. I did not wait for anybody but arose and began by saying that I knew that religion was from God. I went on and told such parts of my experience as it seemed important to me to tell."* His unaffected, Spirit-filled testimony took a deep hold on the people. A blatant unbeliever arose, pressed through the crowd and went out, leaving his hat. A fellow lawyer went out saying, *"He is in earnest, there is no mistake; but he is deranged, that is clear."*

Thereupon the pastor arose to make humble confession that he had not had the faith to believe that Finney would be converted. The service was a long and blessed one.

In the fiery glow of his transforming experience, Finney gave himself tirelessly to testifying for the Savior. The work spread among all classes and extended itself not only through the village but also out to the countryside in every direction. He said at the time,

> My heart was so full that for more than a week I did not feel at all inclined to sleep or eat. I seemed literally to have meat to eat that the world knew nothing of. I did not feel the need of food or of sleep. My mind was full of the love of God to overflowing. . . . The Word of God had wonderful power; and I was every day surprised to find that a few words spoken to an individual would stick in his heart like an arrow.

Shortly afterward the flaming witness for Christ had opportunity to visit his own hometown of Henderson. Of his family, only the youngest brother had ever made a profession of Christ. Finney was met by his father at the gate, and it was here that he responded to his greeting: *"I am well, Father, body and soul. But, Father, you are an old man; all your children have grown up and have left your house; and I never heard a prayer in [your] house."* Thereupon his father burst into tears and bade his son come into the house to pray, with the result that the parents were deeply moved and shortly afterward converted. Then he went with his younger brother to a union service held by Baptists and Congregationalists in that locality, and the Spirit of God came in such power that for a long time none could arise from his knees but only weep, confess, and remain in total submission before the Lord.

The dynamic of God's Spirit upon Finney the first days of his Christian experience was true throughout the length of his ministry. In his *Memoirs*, we read frequent references such as, *"The Spirit was poured out, and before the week ended all the meetings were thronged. . . ."* At Evans Mills, where his public ministry began, he recalled, *"The Holy Spirit was upon me, and I felt confi-*

dent that when the time came for action I should know what to preach. . . . *The Spirit of God came upon me with such power that for more than an hour the Word of God came through me to them. . . .*" When much later in life the work at Oberlin was begun, it is recorded, *"The Holy Spirit fell upon the congregation in a most remarkable manner. A large number of persons dropped their heads, and some groaned so that they could be heard throughout the house. It cut through the false hopes of deceived professors on every side."*

One can, therefore, well understand Finney's earnest and incisive comments, given not unkindly, about his pastor, who had been unable to help the young lawyer in his spiritual life:

> If he was ever converted to Christ, he failed to receive that divine anointing of the Holy Spirit that would give him power in the pulpit and in society for the conversion of souls. Without the direct teaching of the Holy Spirit, a man will never make much progress in preaching the gospel. His speculations and theories will come far short.

Without the Holy Spirit, Finney could do nothing, and neither can we.

Prayer That Prevails

From the very outset of his service for Christ, Finney began to learn the importance and power of prevailing prayer. Of the very earliest days in Adams he could say,

> I used to spend a great deal of time in prayer; sometimes, I thought, literally praying without ceasing. I also found it very profitable, and felt much inclined to hold frequent days of private fasting. On those days I would seek to be entirely alone with God and would generally wander off into the woods or go to the meetinghouse, or somewhere away by myself.

In those early experiences of communion with God, Finney learned the mistake of looking into his own heart and examining his own feelings as he and others were taught to do. By introspection, he made no spiritual advance; by turning his attention to the Lord Jesus Christ and letting the Spirit have his way, he found blessing, instruction, and guidance, so that he could say, *"I found I could not live without enjoying the presence of God; and if at any time a cloud came over me, I could not rest, I could not study, I could not attend to anything with the least satisfaction or benefit until the way was again clear between my soul and God."*

He came to know the reality of deep travail of soul, the prayer that takes hold of the promises of God despite all the attacks of the Enemy. On learning of the desperate physical plight of Judge Wright's sister-in-law, who was not a Christian, the burden of prayer rested so heavily on Finney that it seemed it would crush him. For a long time he was alone in his room before God and could only groan and weep, without being able to express his need in words. Finally he was able to roll the burden on the Lord and obtain assurance that the woman would not die that night or ever die in her sins. One is not surprised, therefore, at his words, *"She did recover, and soon after obtained a hope in Christ."*

Perplexed somewhat by his experience, he sought the counsel of an earnest older Christian who was able to explain from the Scriptures what is meant by "the travail of your soul." Many similar experiences came to the young revivalist; and later in his ministry he could tell with greater clarity the reality and intensity of effective intercession. In his *Lectures on Revival*, he devoted several earnest and impassioned messages to the subject of prevailing prayer. He came to know beyond all shadow of doubt the Word that says, "You do not have because you do not ask God" or "You do not receive, because you ask with wrong motives," and "The prayer of a righteous man is powerful and effective" (James 4:2–3; 5:16).

Obedience Is Better Than Sacrifice

He learned that obedience to the revealed will of God must be immediate, implicit, and irrevocable. In the moment of his conversion he knew that he was called to preach the gospel. When he first came under conviction of the Spirit, the thought occurred to him that if he were to become a Christian, he might have to leave the legal profession and be a preacher. The very thought of leaving his law practice, which was dear to him, was a stumbling block, until he was saved; then he could say,

> After receiving the baptism of the Spirit, I was quite willing to preach the gospel. In fact, I found that I was unwilling to do anything else. I had no longer any desire to practice law. . . . I had no disposition to make money. I had no hungering and thirsting after worldly pleasures and amusements in any direction. My whole mind was taken up with Jesus and His salvation; and the world seemed to me of very little consequence. Nothing, it seemed to me, could be put in competition with the worth of a soul, and no labor, I thought, could be so sweet and no employment so exalted as that of holding up Christ to a dying world.

When he began his public ministry, he had no thought of going to larger villages and cities, but rather of devoting his entire time to the neglected backwoods areas. Again and again in his *Memoirs*, we find that he followed no prearranged plan but was led by the Spirit of God from one settlement to another, often staying for weeks.

Shortly after his wedding in October 1824, he went to Evans Mills for a second series of revival services, with the thought that he would return home within a week in order to bring his bride to his new field of labor. But the revival spread mightily from Evans Mills in various directions, so that the young preacher was led to spend some time in small settlements such as Perch River and Brownsville, and later at Gouverneur, with the result that he wrote to his bride of a few days that he could not return for her until the winter was past. Though not an indifferent lover, Finney's supreme devotion was to the Lord Jesus Christ. Even on his trip home for his wife in the spring of 1825, he was delayed by a revival at Le Rayville, a tiny place south of Evans Mills, where he had stopped to have his horse shod.

Already he had been away from his bride for six months, with little opportunity for exchange of letters because of the primitive conditions of the postal service in those days, but when urged to preach at Le Rayville that afternoon, he went obediently to the schoolhouse for the service. One does not wonder, therefore, at what transpired.

> While I preached, the Spirit of God came down with great power upon the people. So great and manifest was the outpouring of the Spirit that . . . I concluded to spend the night there and preach again in the evening. But the work increased more and more, and in the evening I appointed another meeting in the morning, and in the morning I appointed another in the evening, and soon saw that I would not be able to go any farther after my wife. I told a brother that if he would take my horse and cutter and go after my wife, I would remain. He did so, and I went on preaching from day to day, and from night to night; and there was a powerful revival.

That kind of obedience marked Finney's long and effective ministry of evangelism. For him the center of God's will was of greater importance than society or success or even the sweetness and shelter of home. God's kingdom had first place in his heart.

Until the sunset of his life, Finney continued that same deep, sweet yieldedness to all the will of God. The Enemy came often with strong temptations to turn him back from the Cross and the way of the Crucified, only to find the old warrior of God standing steadfast in his consecration to the divine command. To his heavenly Father he could say without hesitation, *"Yes, I take nothing back. I have no reason for taking anything back; I went no farther in pledges and professions than was reasonable,"* with the result that he could testify, *"Nothing troubled me. I was neither elated nor depressed; I was neither joyful nor sorrowful. My confidence in God was perfect, my acceptance of His will was perfect, and my mind was as calm as heaven."* Such obedience honors the Most High, who said, "Those who honor me will I honor."

Service Has Its Sorrows

Conspicuous among the lessons learned by the great evangelist in the many years of his service was the truth that effectiveness and usefulness in the extension of God's work spawns certain envy and opposition in many, both the sinner and the saved. One rather expects violent opposition from unbelievers, especially those whose economic or social interests are affected by the gospel or who are under the conviction of God's Spirit. The Acts of the Apostles give many examples of the opposition raised against Paul and his helpers in the form of brutal beatings and a dungeon in Philippi, a riot in Ephesus raised by the silversmith whose making of idols was being undermined, and the rage of the multitude in Jerusalem's temple.

In Evans Mills, the first place of his evangelistic service, Finney felt he should bring the interested congregation to a point of decision, and when he thus pressed them, *"They began to look angry and arose en masse and started for the door."* One old infidel of the village, in the midst of his opposition and railing, fell out of his chair at home in a fit of apoplexy and stammered out his last words, *"Don't let Finney pray over my corpse."* An enraged husband of a believing wife swore that he would kill the revivalist and went to the service with a loaded pistol. The would-be murderer came under the pungent conviction of God's Spirit and in the midst of the sermon fell to the floor crying that he was sinking into hell. Some friends helped him home, and after a sleepless night he went out into the woods where he could pour out his heart to God, and there found forgiveness for his sins.

Threats of tar and feathers and riding on a rail were not infrequent in Finney's early experience in backwoods areas and pioneer communities. In the settled and aristocratic cities along the Eastern Seaboard, there were repeated efforts at more refined forms of physical violence. He came to know what Paul meant when he said, "All that will live godly in Christ Jesus will suffer persecution."

Far more subtle and dangerous was the opposition from professing Christians. At the very outset of his witnessing for Christ in his own community, Finney proposed to the young people that they join in a concert of prayer for revival and that each should pray at sunrise, at noon, and at sunset. Afterward he organized a daily prayer meeting that met before daybreak, with the result that revival power came to the community. Then he began to learn to his sorrow that the older members of the church found fault with him and this new movement among the new converts: *"They were jealous of it. They did not know what to make of it, and felt that the young converts were out of place being so forward and so urgent upon the older members of the church. This state of mind finally grieved the Spirit of God."*

Not infrequently denominational differences would create antagonism to the message of evangelism. At Gouverneur, in the very early days, Finney learned that *"as soon as the revival broke out (among Presbyterians) and attracted general attention, the Baptist brethren began to oppose it. They spoke against it and used very objectionable means to arrest its progress. This encouraged a group of young men to join hands in opposition to the work."* It was necessary for Finney's prayer helper, Brother Nash, to rebuke the young men very sharply before they began to break down before the Lord and the opposition dissipated.

Without doubt, the bitterest experience suffered by Finney and his friends came from the opposition headed by outstanding evangelicals such as the Connecticut evangelist Asahel Nettleton and Dr. Lyman Beecher of Boston. Nettleton was the leading revivalist among the Calvinistic Presbyterians and Congregational churches. A graduate of Yale College in the revival days under

President Timothy Dwight, he ministered long and effectively in New England and New York. By temperament and training, Nettleton was quiet, unassuming, reserved. The "new measures," allegedly adopted by Finney and reported adversely by Finney's critics in middle New York State, were to Nettleton a source of alarm.

Nettleton's biographer, Dr. Bennet Tyler, presents the picture of the difficulty from Nettleton's point of view:

> In the year 1826, there was a great religious excitement in the central and western parts of the state of New York, occasioned principally by the labors of the Reverend Charles G. Finney, an evangelist of great zeal and of considerable native eloquence. He had been a lawyer, and having been, as he hoped, converted to Christ, he entered the ministry with little preparatory study. He was bold, ardent, and denunciatory in his manner. He rebuked with harshness and great severity not only open transgressors and impenitent sinners of every description but also professors of religion and ministers of the gospel; and was not infrequently very pointed and personal in his prayers. The consequence was that he was not only met with violent opposition from the open enemies of religion, but many of the most judicious ministers and private Christians felt unwilling to sanction his proceedings. Others became his warm friends and adherents, and imbibing the same spirit, denounced their brethren as "cold and dead and enemies of revivals."

The principal basis for criticism seems to have been the boldness of Finney's preaching and the consequent excitement among the people—in contrast to the quietness of Nettleton's ministry—and also factors such as a spirit of denunciation that was alleged to divide churches, a familiarity in prayer that seemed to be "irreverent" to some doctors of divinity, and "new measures," such as "the practice of females praying in promiscuous assemblies" and of having the "anxious seat" to which those under conviction might come to personal faith and prayer. To Nettleton and Beecher and others, Finney was an innovator and disturber of the peace, one who, in their opinion, threatened to destroy revivals by extravagances and divisions.

The story, as told in the *Memoirs*, gives it as Nettleton, Beecher, and Finney each saw it. It would appear that much of the information given to Finney's critics came from William R. Weeks, pastor of the Congregational church at Paris Hill, New York, an advocate of such extreme determinism in the sovereignty of God that he held that both sin and holiness were produced by a direct act of Almighty Power, and that God made men sinners or holy according to His sovereign will by an act as irresistible as that of Creation itself. Because of opposition to his views on the part of many, Weeks was forced to withdraw from the presbytery of his area and form an association of his own. He was a voluminous correspondent, with letters and reports going in all directions. At the same time, scurrilous printed material about Finney began to appear, such as the pamphlet written by a member of the Unitarian church at Trenton, New York, whose contents can be imagined from the title page, which stated:

A
BUNKER HILL CONTEST
A.D. 1826
Between the "Holy Alliance," for the Establishment
of Hierarchy and Ecclesiastical Domination
over the Human Mind
ON THE ONE SIDE,
And the Asserters of Free Inquiry, Bible Religion,
Christian Freedom and Civil Liberty
ON THE OTHER

THE REV. CHARLES FINNEY,
"Home Missionary" and High Priest of the Alliance
in the Interior of New York.
Headquarters: County of Oneida

When Finney arrived in Auburn, New York, for revival services, he became aware of the opposition and the espionage being carried on. He portrayed vividly his reaction in his description of the deep dealing of God with his soul:

> I said nothing publicly or, as I recollect, privately to anybody on the subject, but gave myself to prayer. I looked to God with great earnestness day after day to be directed; asking Him to show me the path of duty and to give me grace to ride out the storm.
>
> I shall never forget what a scene I passed through one day in my room at Dr. Lansing's. The Lord showed me as in a vision what was before me. He drew so near to me while I was in prayer that my flesh literally trembled. I shook from head to foot, under a full sense of the presence of God. At first, and for some time, it seemed more like being on the top of Sinai amid its full thunderings than in the presence of the cross of Christ.
>
> Never in my life, that I recall, was I so awed and humbled before God as then. Nevertheless, instead of feeling like fleeing, I seemed drawn nearer and nearer to God—nearer to that Presence that filled me with such unutterable awe and trembling. After a season of great humiliation before Him, there came a great lifting up. God assured me that He would be with me and uphold me; that no opposition should prevail against me; that I had nothing to do in regard to all this matter but to keep about my work and wait for the salvation of God.
>
> The sense of God's presence and all that passed between God and my soul at that time, I can never describe. It led me to be perfectly trustful, perfectly calm, and to have nothing but the most perfectly kind feelings toward all the brethren that were misled and were arraying themselves against me. I felt assured that all would come out right, that my true course was to leave everything to God and to keep about my work; and as the storm gathered and the opposition increased, I never for one moment doubted how it would result. I was never disturbed by it, never spent a waking hour thinking of it; when, to all outward appearance, it seemed as if all the churches of the land, except where I had labored, would unite to shut me out of their pulpits.

The deep experience of the prophet Jeremiah as described in chapter 20, verses 7 through 12, was made a blessing to the bewildered yet trusting evangelist. Later in the year, in Troy, New York, Finney had opportunity to meet the older and widely experienced Nettleton, and of the interview held with him, said,

> At that time he could have molded me at discretion; but he said not a word to me about my manner of conducting revivals, nor did he ever write a word to me upon the subject. He kept me at arm's length; and although, as I have said, we conversed on some points of theology then much discussed, it was plain that he was unwilling to say anything regarding revivals, and would not allow me to accompany him to the meeting.

Nettleton's biographer states that there were two interviews with Finney, held with a view to bringing the men into harmony and cooperation, but in them Nettleton was painfully disappointed:

> He found that Mr. Finney was unwilling to abandon certain measures that he had regarded as exceedingly calamitous to the cause of revivals, and which, of course, he could not sanction. He perceived also that there could be no hope of convincing Mr. Finney of his errors, so long as he was upheld and encouraged by ministers of high respectability.

In July 1827, after much correspondence between Nettleton, Beecher, and other church leaders, a conference was held in New Lebanon, New York, with the intent of clarifying the whole matter. Beecher and Nettleton seemed unwilling to allow preachers who had been in Finney's revivals to speak on behalf of the methods of the evangelist and the results of his ministry, but the objection was overruled. A long and detailed "historical letter" by Nettleton, which had been circulated among his friends and later published to the consternation of many, was read, to which Finney made reply that none of the facts mentioned therein was true, adding: *"All the brethren are here with whom I have performed all these labors, and they know whether I am chargeable with any of these things in any of their congregations. If they know or believe that any of these things are true of me, let them say so here and now."*

The conference, which had no official standing, prepared some resolutions of a general nature about the revivals and then dispersed. Lyman Beecher, in his *Memoirs*, declares that he said, *"Finney, I know your plan, and you know I do; you mean to come to Connecticut, and carry a streak of fire to Boston. But if you attempt it, as the Lord liveth, I'll meet you at the state line and call out all the artillery men and fight every inch of the way to Boston, and then I'll fight you there."* For his part, Finney declares he does not remember any such statement, nor did he have any design or desire to go to Connecticut or to Boston. The following year a group of clergymen assembled in Philadelphia discussed the difficulty and drew up a resolution to the effect that further correspondence and controversy would only harm the cause of Christ.

The controversy was a source of deep regret and sorrow to Finney and to his critics as well. Toward the end of his life, Finney said,

> As I have labored extensively in this country and in Great Britain, and no exceptions have been made to my measures, it has been assumed and asserted that since the opposition made by Mr. Nettleton and Dr. Beecher, I have been reformed and have given up the measures they complained of. This is an entire mistake. I have always and everywhere used all the measures I used in those revivals, and have often added other measures whenever I have deemed it expedient. I have seen the necessity of reformation in this respect. Were I to live my life over again, I think that with the experience of more than forty years in revival labors, I should, under the same circumstances, use substantially the same measures as I did then.

Criticism of a big man by his smaller fellows is among the most common experiences in life. Moses, the lawgiver, faced the carping criticism of princes like Dathan and Abiram, and even of his brother Aaron and sister Miriam. The apostle Paul knew what it was to have all the Christians in Asia Minor turn away from him. Who has been more maligned than Martin Luther or John Wesley? The saintly and scholarly Jonathan Edwards was driven from his church in Northampton after many years of labor. The Lord Jesus knew the biting sarcasm of His brothers and neighbors and could well state that the servant is not above his master. Finney's foes made many belittling and bewildering criticisms, such as the ridiculous statement that the evangelist claimed to be the "brigadier general" of the Lord. The story had wide circulation and in an interesting manner boomeranged against one who had believed it. Lewis Tappan, a Unitarian layman of Boston and a leading merchant, was told the tale by a clergyman of his church and repeated it to his brother Arthur and others in New York City. The brother, an earnest Christian businessman, declared it to be untrue and asked for the evidence that Lewis was sure could be forthcoming. When no evidence came, despite a large reward, Lewis Tappan was deeply disturbed and disappointed. Later he came under Finney's preaching and was soundly converted. He then became "as firm and zealous in his support of orthodox views and revivals of religion as he had been in his opposition to them."

Revival Requires a Tender Heart

Preeminent among the lessons learned by Finney was the need for personal devotions in daily Bible reading and prayer and the need of perennial, personal revival in the breaking of his own heart. He had begun to read the Bible occasionally before he was converted, but after that transforming experience, he became an avid student of the sacred Scriptures. Of his early Christian days, when perplexed by dogmas that did not seem to have scriptural basis, he could say,

Often when I left Mr. Gale, I would go to my room and

spend a long time on my knees over my Bible. Indeed, I read my Bible on my knees a great deal during those days of conflict, beseeching the Lord to teach me His own mind on these points. I had nowhere to go but directly to the Bible and to the philosophy or workings of my own mind.

Throughout his life Finney had a deep longing for fellowship with the Most High and for complete conformity to His will. Opposition was created to his views on sanctification as a present experience in the life of the Christian, but Finney moved onward with God. During one winter when he was at the Broadway Tabernacle in New York City and absent from the classes in Oberlin, he had a season of deep and sweet refreshing, which he described in earnestness and eloquence:

> After a season of great searching of heart, He brought me, as He has often done, into a large place, and gave me much of that divine sweetness of my soul, of which President Edwards speaks as it came in his own experience. That winter I had a thorough breaking up; so much so that sometimes, for a considerable period, I could not refrain from loud weeping in view of my own sin and of the love of God in Christ.

Some years later, while preaching in Boston, he recalls in his *Memoirs*:

> The Lord gave my own soul a very thorough overhauling and a fresh baptism of His Spirit. . . . I gave myself to a great deal of prayer. After my evening services, I would retire as early as I could, but rose at four o'clock in the morning because I could sleep no longer, and immediately went to the study and engaged in prayer. . . . My days were spent, so far as I could get time, in searching the Scriptures; I read nothing all that winter but my Bible; and a great deal of it seemed new to me. . . . The whole Scripture seemed to be all ablaze with light, and not only light, but it seemed as if God's Word was ingrained with the very life of God.

In those days there came a profound desire to search out his heart and to test his consecration to all the will of God. It was at that time that Finney had the soul-searching struggle of a deeper consecration than ever before, which included his dear wife and family. With utter and unreserved yielding to all that the will of God might be, he came to a perfect resting in that will as he had never known before.

> At this time it seemed as if my soul was wedded to Christ in a sense in which I had never had any thought or concept before. The language of the Song of Solomon was as natural to me as my breath. I thought I could understand well the state of mind he was in when he wrote that song; and concluded then, as I have ever thought since, that that song was written after he had been reclaimed from his great backsliding. I not only had all the freshness of my first love but a vast increase to it. Indeed, the Lord lifted me so far above anything that I had ever experienced before, and taught me so much of the meaning of the Bible, of Christ's power and faithfulness, that I often found myself saying to Him, *"I had not known or conceived that any such thing was true."* I then realized what is meant by the saying, "He is able to do exceeding abundantly above all that we ask or think." He did at that time teach me infinitely above all that I had ever asked or thought. I had had no concept of the length and breath, and height and depth, and efficiency of his grace.

After that meeting with his Master, there never came again to Finney the great struggles and protracted seasons of agonizing prayer over the will of God; rather he had come to a calmness and perfect confidence in the fulfillment of the divine will, and to say,

> He enables me now to rest in Him and let everything sink into His perfect will, with much more readiness than ever before the experience of that winter. I have felt since then a religious freedom, a religious buoyancy and delight in God and in His Word, a steadiness of faith, a Christian liberty and overflowing love that I had only experienced, I may say, occasionally before. . . . It seems to me that I can find God within me

in such a sense that I can rest upon Him and be quiet, lay my heart in His hands, nestle down in His perfect will, and have no worry or anxiety.

Some years later there came the supreme testing of His confidence in God. When the call home came to his wife, God's servant could say, despite the deep affliction, "I did not feel any murmuring or the least resistance to the will of God." The Lord was pleased to make real to him the ineffable bliss of heaven enjoyed by his departed life partner, so that heaven became very real and wonderful to him in his grief.

Finney learned that only a few seem to understand the experience of rest in God:

> But in preaching, I have found that nowhere can I preach those truths on which my own soul delights to live, and be understood, except it be by a very small number. I have never found that more than a very few, even of my own people, appreciate and receive those views of God and Christ, and the fullness of His free salvation, upon which my own soul still delights to feed.

———

Finney was always a man of the people, but in a larger sense, he was a man of God. He was almost constantly among people to witness to them of God's saving grace, to help them, to teach them, and at the same time his own heart was drawn close to the Most High. Always active and aggressive in service for his fellowmen, he was in reality also in a fellowship with God that filled his own soul with awe, wonder, and power. His spirit drank from the hidden springs of salvation like the man of the first psalm who, making his delight in the law of the Lord and meditating day and night therein, became like a tree planted by rivers of water.

The rugged regimen of life sweetened rather than soured him. The stern lessons of human hatred of the gospel and those who proclaim it drove him to his knees and to his Bible, there to find the knowledge of the Crucified One, who, in the days of His flesh, had been a man of sorrows and acquainted with grief. Like his Master, Finney was loved by many and also misunderstood and misrepresented by many. Misrepresentation did not intimidate him, nor did misunderstanding bewilder him. He was ever learning, ever going onward with God, persuaded with the apostle Paul that "no eye has seen, no ear has heard, no mind has conceived what God has prepared for those who love him—but God has revealed it to us by his Spirit" (1 Corinthians 2:9–10).

3

The Multitudes Revive

When Finney was converted at the age of twenty-nine, he had never been in a revival nor attended an evangelistic service. In fact, prior to his coming to Adams three years earlier, he had attended religious services only infrequently. So dynamic and transforming was his experience of faith in Christ that he immediately became a witness for the Savior, first among his neighbors and friends, then his family; and after a year or more of personal work, coupled with much prayer and Bible study, he began his public ministry.

As indicated earlier, he had no intention of entering formally into the ministry as pastor of a settled church; rather, he felt called to the backwoods areas that were quite neglected. For more than three years he labored in small suburbs in west-central New York, villages whose names have disappeared or have been completely obscured in the development of the Empire State. Led by God's Spirit, he devoted long periods of time to tiny places like Evans Mills, Antwerp, Gouverneur, and Western, before being called to Rome, Utica, Auburn, and Troy.

After the conference on "New Measures" held in New Lebanon

in 1826, Finney, under the urgent invitation of earnest Christian people desiring revival, began to move in larger cities. From 1827 to 1829 he was in Wilmington and Philadelphia, and the following year he held his first revival services in New York City. Later, in 1830, he led the first great revival efforts in Rochester, a city he visited also in 1842 and 1855. On each occasion he felt an unexplainable aversion to going to Rochester, even though he greatly admired the thriving young city and loved its people; only after overcoming his inward misgivings did he go there and realize great evangelistic triumphs. It was as though the Enemy of man's soul was determined to prevent Finney's preaching the gospel in Rochester.

He was in New England in 1831—first in Providence, and later in Boston, by invitation of Dr. Lyman Beecher and other pastors. Finney became greatly attached to the "Hub of the Universe," as it was called, and on four subsequent occasions held protracted meetings in that citadel of Unitarianism. The winter of 1841–42 became known as the time of "The Great Boston Revival," during which the Baptist evangelist Elder Jacob Knapp and also Edward N. Kirk held revival services simultaneously with those of Finney. A part of the difficulty faced during the Boston campaign was the excitement aroused by the Millerites, who were alarming the people of New England with the assertion that the Second Coming of Christ would occur on April 23, 1843. During the same winter, William Ellery Channing, the great Unitarian leader, was in his declining days when he became deeply interested in Finney's revivalism. He expressed to one of his parishioners a desire to converse with Finney, but died while visiting in Vermont before he had the opportunity to see him. After the campaign in Boston in 1843, subsequent revivals were held in 1856–57 and 1858–59.

To return to the chronology, in 1832 Finney became pastor of the Chatham Street Chapel in New York City, which in time developed into the Broadway Tabernacle. It was at that time that Finney finally broke with the Presbyterian Church, which had ordained him, and the new Broadway Tabernacle was organized along Congregational lines. His pastorate continued until 1837.

It was during his ministry in New York City that he delivered the "Lectures on Revival," given after he had spent several months in the Mediterranean to recuperate his health. In 1835 he accepted the invitation to serve as professor of theology at the new college in Oberlin, Ohio. The college classes were held in the summertime, which gave the fall and winter for Finney's ministry in New York City.

After resigning his New York pastorate, he became interim pastor of the church in Oberlin for a time, as well as professor of theology. Later he assumed the full pastorate of the church, and although he had to be away on frequent evangelistic efforts, he remained pastor of the church until 1872. In 1851 he was called to the presidency of Oberlin College, and continued in that capacity for fourteen years. When he relinquished his administrative duties in 1865, the college had grown in numbers and strength, despite the trying days of the War Between the States. There were revival efforts in new and older areas in the United States, such as Cleveland, Cincinnati, Detroit, Hartford, and Syracuse, as well as returns to numerous places of previous campaigns. Twice Finney labored extensively in the British Isles, first in 1849–50, and later in 1858–59. On this latter occasion he went to Britain with the hope that the tremendous dynamic of the revivals in 1857 and 1858 in the United States would be transmitted beyond the Atlantic. He was not disappointed.

What justification is there for the claim that Finney was America's preeminent revivalist? No account of his life, however brief and limited, should omit entirely some of the record of revivals held under his leadership. His *Memoirs* gives a very full and interesting account of his evangelistic efforts and makes his autobiography a perennial good seller.[1] Following are some of the high points of his service, in places large and small.

With almost no formal training but with much Bible study and

---

[1] See his autobiography, condensed and edited by Helen Wessel and published by Bethany House.

prayer, he began his ministry at Evans Mills and Antwerp, small communities in northern Jefferson County, New York. The church historian William Warren Sweet, in his *Revivalism in America*,[2] summarizes the advent of Finney onto the American scene by declaring, "Evans Mills and Antwerp were rough, uncouth communities, but immediately under the vivid preaching of the ex-lawyer/preacher a wave of revivalism began to sweep through the whole region. He preached outdoors, in barns, and in schoolhouses. Thus began one of the most remarkable careers in the history of modern revivalism."

The newly appointed pioneer missionary began his service in fairly poor health, but travel on horseback, incessant labors in God's service, and aggressive evangelism seemed to have cured him of incipient tuberculosis. When there was little response to his first messages, he pressed his audience for a decision, only to find growing opposition, even threats of tar and feathers. Prayer by himself and with "Praying Nash" turned the spiritual tide, and the people of the countryside, casting aside their harvesting implements, crowded into schoolhouses and churches to receive the Savior. When invited to preach in a rural community entirely unknown to him, even as to its name, Finney felt led to preach on "Lot Fleeing From Sodom," only to find the neighborhood known popularly as "Sodom" because of its wickedness and his host known as "Lot." One hardly wonders that his message was first of all received with fierce antagonism, but soon the "slain of the Lord" were many.

The revivals in the area of Western, a community near Rome, New York, began to attract rather widespread interest. On arriving in that vicinity, Finney was invited to a prayer service that proved to be extremely dull and discouraging. When the visiting revivalist rose to speak and declared their prayer meeting to have been a mockery, one can understand the anger of his listeners. When it appeared that the gathering would be broken up, the lay-

---

[2]William Warren Sweet, *Revivalism in America* (New York: Scribner's Sons, 1944).

leader burst into tears and fell on his knees to pray. Finney recalled, *"Every man and woman went down upon their knees . . . they all wept and confessed and broke their hearts before God. This scene continued for an hour; a more thorough breaking down and confession I have seldom witnessed. The result was that revival ran throughout the community and whole families were converted."*

For a year and a half Finney labored in Philadelphia, the first large city on the Eastern Seaboard to witness the "new evangelism" from western New York. The converts were numerous in every part of the city, but we have no record of the extent of the revival. An unusual and signal demonstration of the power of God was evangelism among the lumbermen who came to the city from the headwaters of the Delaware River to sell their large rafts of logs. They came from a rough, unsettled, and largely unoccupied area without schools or churches. Of them Finney recalls in his *Memoirs*:

> These men that come down with lumber attended our meetings, and quite a number of them were hopefully converted. They went back into the wilderness and began to pray for the outpouring of the Holy Spirit, and to tell the people around them what they had seen in Philadelphia, and to exhort them to attend to their salvation. Their efforts were immediately blessed, and the revival began to take hold and to spread among those lumbermen. It went on in a most powerful and remarkable manner. It spread to such an extent that in many cases persons would be convicted and converted who had not attended any meetings and who were almost as ignorant as heathen. Men who were cutting out lumber and were living in little shanties alone, or where two or three or more were together, would be seized with such conviction that it would lead them to wander off and inquire what they should do; and they would be converted, and thus the revival spread. The greatest simplicity was manifested by the converts.
>
> I have said that this work began in the spring of 1829. In the spring of 1831 I was at Auburn again. Two or three men from this lumber region came there to see me and to inquire

how they could get some ministers to go in there. They said that no less than five thousand people had been converted in that lumber region and that the revival had extended itself for eighty miles without a single minister of the gospel there.

I have never been in that region, but from all I have ever heard about it, I have regarded it as one of the most remarkable revivals that has occurred in this country. It was carried on almost independently of the ministry, among a class of people very ignorant in regard to all ordinary instruction; and yet so clear and wonderful were the teachings of God that I have always understood the revival was remarkably free from fanaticism or wildness or anything objectionable.

The three revival efforts in Rochester constitute possibly the high-water mark of Finney's effectiveness. He went to the service with an inward reluctance, only to find tremendous response to the gospel. It was in Rochester that he was first led to designate the "anxious seat," where the penitent could come for prayer. When the Spirit of God began to move multitudes to a deep sense of conviction for sin and then to saving faith in the Lord Jesus, there came many from all classes of society, but chiefly from among the professionals and merchants. A student in Rochester Academy, Charles P. Bush, later to become a leading pastor in New York City, was led to the Savior under Finney's ministry, and wrote of that first revival in his native city:

> The whole community was stirred. Religion was the topic of conversation in the house, in the shop, in the office, and on the street. . . . The only theater in the city was converted into a livery stable, the only circus into a soap and candle factory. Grog shops were closed; the Sabbath was honored; the sanctuaries were thronged with happy worshipers; a new impulse was given to every philanthropic enterprise; the fountains of benevolence were opened, and men lived to do good.
>
> It is worth noting that a large number of the leading men of the place were among the converts—the lawyers, the judges, physicians, merchants, bankers, and master mechanics. These

classes were more moved from the very first than any other. Tall oaks were bowed as by the blast of the hurricane. Skeptics and scoffers were brought in, and a large number of the most promising young men. It is said that no less than forty of them entered the ministry.

It is not too much to say that the whole character of the city was changed by that revival. Most of the leaders of society being converted, and exerting a controlling influence in social life, in business, and in civil affairs, religion was enthroned as it has been in few places. . . . Even the courts and the prisons bore witness to its blessed effects. There was a wonderful falling off in crime. The courts had little to do, and the jail was nearly empty for years afterward.

The magnitude of the revival efforts can be surmised only from Finney's quiet word:

> The greatness of the work at Rochester at that time attracted so much attention of ministers and Christians throughout the state of New York, throughout New England, and in many parts of the United States, that the very fame of it was an efficient instrument in the hands of the Spirit of God in promoting the greatest revival of religion throughout the land that this country had ever witnessed. Years after this, in conversing with Dr. Beecher about this powerful revival and its results, he remarked, "That was the greatest work of God, and the greatest revival of religion, that the world has ever seen in so short a time. One hundred thousand," he remarked, "were reported as having connected themselves with churches as the result of that great revival. This," he said, "is unparalleled in the history of the church, and of the progress of religion." He spoke of this having been done in one year; and said that in no year during the Christian era had we any account of so great a revival of religion.

The two later revival efforts in Rochester were also crowned with outstanding success. In each effort the greatest impression from the very outset was made in the upper classes of society. Of the last effort in that beloved city, perhaps the favorite of Finney, it could be written:

> There were many very striking cases of conversion in this revival, as in the revival that preceded it. The work spread and excited so much interest that it became the general topic of conversation throughout the city and the surrounding region of country. Merchants arranged to have their clerks attend—a part of them one day, and a part the next day. The work became so general throughout the city that in all places of public resort, in stores and public houses, in banks, in the street and in public conveyances, and everywhere, the work of salvation that was going on was the absorbing topic.
>
> Men that had stood out in the former revivals, many of them bowed to Christ in this. Some men who had been open Sabbath-breakers, others that had been openly profane, indeed, all classes of persons, from the highest to the lowest, from the richest to the poorest, were visited by the power of this revival and brought to Christ. I continued there throughout the winter, the revival increasing continually to the last. Rev. Dr. Anderson, president of the university, engaged in the work with great cordiality, and, as I understood, a large number of the students in the university were converted at that time. The pastors of the two Baptist churches took hold of the effort, and I preached several times in their churches.

During the nationwide revival of 1857–58, Finney was in New York and Boston, and rejoiced in the magnitude of God's work in those stirring days. That winter, he declared,

> This will be remembered as the time when a great revival prevailed throughout all the northern states. It swept over the land with such power that for a time it was estimated that not less than fifty thousand conversions occurred in a single week. This revival had some very peculiarly interesting features. It was carried on to a large extent through lay influence, so much so as almost to cast the ministers into the shadows. A daily prayer meeting had been observed in Boston for several years;

and in the autumn previous to the great outburst, the daily prayer meeting had been established on Fulton Street, New York, which has continued to this day. Indeed, daily prayer meetings were established throughout the length and breadth of the northern states. I recollect in one of our prayer meetings in Boston that winter that a gentleman arose and said, "I am from Omaha, Nebraska. On my journey East, I have found a continuous prayer meeting all the way. We say it is about two thousand miles from Omaha to Boston; and here was a prayer meeting about two thousand miles in extent."

When Mr. and Mrs. Finney first went to England, in the autumn of 1849, Americans were not especially welcome in the British Isles. Hardly a generation had passed since hostility between the two countries had ceased, and during the intervening decades there had been high contempt for the frontier customs of the Americans on the part of British travelers, and in return there had been repeated "twisting of the lion's tail" by unduly sensitive Americans. Finney's ministry began in the village of Houghton, where gospel work was at low ebb. A Quaker industrialist, Potto Brown, was instrumental in getting the American revivalist to his neighborhood. He had read *Lectures on Revival* at the encouragement of his pastor and was deeply interested in the temporal and eternal welfare of his employees and neighbors. A revival began at once and spread among all classes and into the neighboring villages. From Houghton the Finneys were invited to Birmingham, where revival ministry was carried on in several churches, *"and there was a powerful revival, such a movement as they had never seen. The revival swept through the congregation with great power, and a very large proportion of the impenitent were turned to Christ."*

Later there came an invitation to Whitefield's Tabernacle in London, of which Dr. John Campbell was then pastor. Finney's ministry began with several weeks of Bible teaching for Christians, until finally the time came for the invitation to "after meetings." In response to Finney's request for an inquiry room, the pastor offered a kindergarten that would accommodate thirty or forty people. The pastor was astonished to learn that Finney wanted a room that would hold several hundred people, and probably partly in amusement—certainly not in faith—he offered a lecture room a city block from the Tabernacle that would accommodate fifteen hundred or more.

The American revivalist made it perfectly clear to his audience that neither professing Christians nor careless sinners were invited to the after meeting. *"Those, and only those, who are not Christians but who are anxious for the salvation of their souls and wish instruction given them directly upon the question of their present duty to God are expected to attend."* Thereupon the regular meeting was dismissed, and those who were "anxious" crowded the way up the street to the appointed inquiry room. The lecture room was soon filled to capacity, quite to the astonishment of the good pastor, who from a window in the church had watched his parishioners go to seek the Savior. Finney explained carefully and forcefully the gospel message to the assembly of seekers, after which all knelt down to commit themselves entirely to the Savior. Finney sought to suppress emotion and outcry in order that everyone might hear the word of the gospel; nevertheless, *"there was a great sobbing and weeping in every part of the house."*

In subsequent meetings, *"the aisles in that house were so narrow and so packed that it was impossible to use what is called the anxious seat, or for people to move about at all in the congregation.... On some occasions, if the house seated as many as was supposed, not less than two thousand people arose when an appeal was made.... Great numbers came every week, and conversions multiplied. People came, as I learned, from every part of the city. Many people walked several miles every Sabbath to attend the meetings."*

The impact of the revival was not confined to the Tabernacle but extended to many congregations in various parts of the city. An Anglican clergyman became so deeply burdened for his congregation that he set about to promote a revival in his large parish. Twenty prayer meetings were established, and the rector gave himself to preaching directly to his people with the result that more than fifteen hundred persons were hopefully converted. Other Anglican churches were likewise partakers of the awakening.

Because of the tremendous revivals in America during the winter of 1857–58, Finney was persuaded that he should go again to Britain. Wherever he ministered in England and Scotland there were great revivals. In Huntington, where there had been no revival up to that time, there came a very deep moving of God's Spirit, which transformed professing Christians and then *"spread extensively among the unconverted and greatly changed the religious aspect of the town."*

Finney preached in Edinburgh and also in Aberdeen in the far north of Scotland, the scene of the great revivals in the days of Robert Murray McCheyne. Later, in the area of Manchester, and especially in Bolton, a manufacturing center near the metropolis, a sweeping revival took place. Union services were held with the Christians of Bolton zealous in advertising the meetings and in visiting the homes with gospel literature. *"All classes of persons, high and low, rich and poor, male and female, became interested. . . . Great numbers would come forward, crowding as best they could through the dense masses that filled every nook and corner of the house. . . . After the inquirers had come forward, we engaged in a prayer meeting, having several prayers in succession while the inquirers knelt before the Lord."*

Finney had opportunity to minister to the employees of a large cotton mill, and in the ensuing awakening nearly everyone came to a saving knowledge of Christ. By the deep searching of God's Spirit, both believers and unbelievers came under conviction of wrongs that had to be made right by restitution. In some cases the amount of money was very considerable. For example, one man returned more than thirty thousand dollars, which he had wrongfully received. The Bolton newspaper, *The Revival*, stated that in one week there were four hundred conversions and, during the entire campaign, two thousand professions.

Some concept of the impact of revivalism under Finney can be gained from perusing excerpts from contemporary accounts. The depth and extent of the nineteenth-century revival movements are quite unknown to us in the twenty-first century, and as we read the account there is stirred deep within us an insatiable longing to the effect, "Oh, God, grant that the days Finney knew may soon come again."

Following is Finney's account of the first awakening in Rochester, and then the words of a contemporary of another denomination, as he wrote in *The American Baptist* magazine.

Finney's Report on Rochester

Soon after our arrival, there were some very marked conversions. The wife of a prominent lawyer in that city was one of the first converts. She was a woman of high standing, of culture and extensive influence. The first time I saw her, a Christian friend of hers had come with her to my room and introduced her.

The woman had been a "woman of the world," and very fond of society. She afterward told me that when I first came there, she greatly regretted it and feared there would be a revival, which would greatly interfere with the pleasures and amusements that she had promised herself that winter. On conversing with her, I found that the Spirit of the Lord was indeed dealing with her in an unsparing manner. She was, in fact, bowed down with great conviction of sin. After considerable conversation with her, I pressed her to renounce sin and the world and self . . . and everything for Christ. I saw that she was a very proud woman, in fact, this struck me as the most marked feature of her character. At the conclusion of our conversation, we knelt down to pray, and my mind being full of the subject of the pride of her heart, I very soon introduced the text, "Except ye be converted, and become as little children, ye shall not enter into the kingdom of heaven" (Matthew 18:3). I turned this subject over in prayer, and almost immediately I heard her, as she was kneeling by my side, repeating the text over and over. I observed that her mind was taken with it, and the Spirit of God was pressing it upon her heart. I therefore continued to pray, holding the subject before her mind and holding her up before God as needing that very thing—to be converted, to become as a little child.

I felt then that the Lord was answering prayer; He was doing the very work that I had asked Him to do. Her heart broke down, her feelings poured forth, and before we rose from our knees she was, indeed, as a little child. When I stopped praying and opened my eyes and looked at her, her face was turned upward and the tears were streaming down. . . . She rose up, became peaceful, and was settled into a joyous faith. From that moment she was outspoken in her religious convictions and zealous for the conversion of her friends. Her conversion, of course, produced much excitement among that class of people to which she belonged. . . .

There was at that time a high school in Rochester, presided over by a young man who was the son of the pastor in Brighton, near Rochester. The young man was a skeptic, but the school he headed was very large and flourishing. His assistant and associate in the school at that time was a Christian woman. The students attended the religious services, and many of them soon became deeply anxious about their souls. One morning the principal found that his classes could not recite for him . . . they were so anxious about their souls that they wept, and it confounded him. He called his associate and told her that the young people were so exercised about their souls that they could not recite . . . and should he send for Mr. Finney to give them instruction? She afterward informed me of this, and said that she was very glad to have him make the inquiry, and most cordially advised him to send for me. He did so, and the revival took tremendous hold of that school. The young man himself was soon hopefully converted, as well as nearly every person in the school. A few years later the school associate informed me that more than forty persons that were converted in that school at the time had become ministers . . . and a large number had become foreign missionaries. . . .

I have said that the moral aspect of things was greatly

changed by this revival. It was a young city, full of enterprise . . . and full of sin. As the revival swept through the town
and converted the great mass of the most influential people,
both men and women, the change in the order, sobriety, and
morality of the city was wonderful. . . .

Finney's Work as Seen by a Contemporary

The recent revivals of religion, as they have been termed,
appear to have commenced in the western part of New York,
in Rochester, and the surrounding region, in the autumn of
1830. During the next three or four months the work spread
rapidly and extended itself over a considerable portion of the
state. In the course of the winter, favorable appearances were
observed in New York City, which at the coming of spring assumed a most cheering and decisive character. Nearly all the
evangelical churches in the city have shared in the revival, and
thousands, it is hoped, have been born of God. While the work
was thus pervading the city and state of New York, it made its
appearance in the western parts of Massachusetts and in various places in Connecticut. At the same time the tokens of
God's presence and power were displayed in some of the principal towns in Maine. About the first of March an unusual
spirit of prayer was imparted to the churches in Boston, and
it began to be apparent that the Lord was there. From that
time, the work has been in progress in Boston and the surrounding region, and many have been made the happy subjects of renewing grace. At the same time that the revival was
extending eastward, it was also spreading to the south and
west. Philadelphia, Charleston, the District of Columbia, Cincinnati, and various places in the middle, southern, and western states have been visited, and in nearly every place in which
the work was begun, it is still in progress. It has been estimated by one who has paid particular attention to the subject,
and has the best means of forming a judgment, that as many
as one thousand congregations in the United States have been
visited within six months, to a greater or lesser extent, with
revivals of religion, and that the whole number of conversions
is probably not less than fifty thousand. Truly this is a great

and glorious work—sufficient to fill the hearts of God's people with humility and gratitude and their mouths with thanksgiving! A work in the promotion of which holy beings on earth and in heaven have combined influences and rejoiced together!

This work derives additional importance from the situation and rank of many of the principal places that have been visited. It is worthy of special notice that those places that have partaken most largely of the blessing are those that exert the greatest influence upon society. Cities and colleges have been the scenes of the deepest interest, as though the divine Spirit would correct the streams of moral influence by purifying the fountains. The colleges that have been most favored are Yale, Amherst, Middlebury, Bowdoin, Williams, Hamilton, Jefferson, Kenyon, Union, Hampden-Sydney, New Jersey, Western Reserve, and the University of Ohio. The number of students who appear to have become converted in these institutions during the present revival is three hundred and twenty. The effects of this change will not be limited to these young people. Hundreds and thousands will doubtless experience in consequence of it a similar change in their character and destiny for eternity, and a multitude that no man can number will rejoice in the result forever.

———

In this work of salvation, individuals of all ranks, ages, and characters have been included. The child of six and seven, yet in elementary school, and the older sinner who has lived forty years in rebellion, have in the same congregation been brought together at the feet of Jesus, as well as some of all the intermediate ages. The great and learned officers of state and the most illiterate servants have been found together in the same prayer meeting on a level before the throne of God. The man of wealth and the poor man have united in begging for mercy of Him who is no respecter of persons. It is, however, believed that no previous revival ever took so large a proportion of the wealth and learning and influence of society as this has done. Literary and professional people who are at the head of society, giving the tone to public sentiment, have been brought into the kingdom in far greater numbers than ever before was known. The morally upright who have regarded themselves as approved of God on account of the purity of their lives, and the openly vicious and profane have been alike humbled before God on account of their vileness and the just sentence of wrath that was upon them. In many instances the intemperate, tottering upon the verge of a drunkard's grave, have been rescued by the sovereign mercy of God. Some of every character and condition in life have been taken, so that we need not despair of any, but should labor and pray in hope and faith for all.

In some congregations, especially in the western section of the state of New York, the work has been so general and thorough that whole customs of society have been changed. . . .

Revival, the gentle breathing of God's Spirit upon the dry bones of a dead orthodoxy or of a defiant godlessness, became a whirlwind in the ministry of Finney. To professing Christians there came a newness of life and an assurance of faith after contrition of spirit and confession of sin. Old churches were revitalized and new ones established; careless sinners were awakened to conviction of their lost condition and to deep and radical conversion. Little children and elderly men, backwoodsmen, farmers, mechanics, lawyers, and merchants crowded into the kingdom of God. Drunkards were transformed, taverns abandoned, churches filled, and jails emptied. Uprightness of conversation and conduct became the accepted standard in American life, from the country merchant behind his crude counter to the lawmaker in the lofty halls of Congress. America was vastly different and better because of the revivals led by Finney and his contemporaries, and the America of today can be transformed by the same power.

———

It should be added for this brief record of his long and useful life that Finney was married three times, and that he found each helpmeet to be indispensable to him in God's service. His life, which had been marked by stress and storm, became the most tranquil near its close. At the conclusion of a very peaceful Lord's Day, on August 16, 1875, in Oberlin, Ohio, he finished his earthly service. For more than half a century he had been a witness to small and great, to illiterate and learned, in pioneer rural America as well as in some of the proud cities of the world, new and old— London, Edinburgh, New York, Boston. He being dead yet speaks to us that revival is the divine method of spreading the good news of salvation in Christ to the earth's multitudes and is the dynamic that can change individuals, nations, and the course of human events.

PART TWO

The Methods

4

The Pattern of Revival

A genuine revival is a wonderful, melding, gracious moving of God's Spirit on a community or a whole country. It is commonly regarded as an act of divine sovereignty allowed by Almighty God at His pleasure and at His direction. Man is generally considered to be utterly incapable of promoting or hindering such a manifestation of sovereign power. But evidence of Christian experience does not bear out the accuracy of such a concept; in fact, it seems to be conclusive that there is much that Christians are to do in the preparation and promotion of true revival. We shall consider the matter from a realistic, practical viewpoint, as made apparent in the experience of God's people in days past.

Is There a "Science of Revival"?

The editor of the 1832 edition of Edwards' *Faithful Narrative and Thoughts on Revival* made this very pertinent observation on the importance of God's people studying the subject of revival so as to better prepare themselves and their fellow countrymen for a mighty outpouring of God's Spirit in quickening, saving power:

It is incumbent, then, upon the church to prepare for such a state of revival as we are thus authorized to anticipate. The subject of revival must be more studied and better understood. And the spirit of revival must be more diligently cultivated. What motivation would at once be given for the study of the art of war if it were anticipated that the country would soon be involved in such a calamity. Why should not *the science of revival*, and the course of action required in revivals, become a matter of general study in the church? Ministers have doubtless much to learn concerning revivals, the signs of their approach, the means of producing them, the manner of conducting them, the way to guard against difficulties, and to secure the happiest results. And every Christian ought to understand revival, because everyone has a part to act in relation to them. There is a growing conviction in the church of the responsibility that rests upon every individual professor of religion in times of revival. It then becomes manifest how much the conduct of each one may help or hinder the effect of divine truth. But without knowledge on the subject, no one can correctly perform his duty. And unless one understands the principles that are applicable in them, it is impossible that he should be well prepared to act in the ever-varying emergencies that a revival does not fail to exhibit. How great the calamity to prevent or destroy a revival from not knowing how to act in regard to it! Or to resist and extinguish a real revival, under a mistaken opinion that it is spurious! Or to encourage and cherish an artificial excitement, supposing it to be a genuine work of the Spirit of God! Or to have the fruits that might have followed a revival stinted or marred by any backward or ill-judged procedures.

Finney is explicit and exacting in his explanation that a revival of religion, as he called it, "is not a miracle" but "the result of the *right* use of the appropriate means." Follow carefully the exposition he gave out of long experience, adapted here for the modern reader.

A revival of religion is not a miracle

1. A miracle is generally defined to be a divine interference, setting aside or suspending the laws of nature. Revival is not a miracle in this sense. All the laws of matter and mind remain in force. They are neither suspended nor set aside in a revival.

2. Revival is not a miracle according to another definition of the term *miracle*: "something above the powers of nature." There is nothing in the promotion of Christianity beyond the ordinary powers of nature. It consists entirely in the *right exercise* of the powers of nature. It is just that and nothing else.

3. It is not a miracle or dependent on a miracle in any sense. It is a purely philosophical result of the right use of the constituted means—as much so as any other effect produced by the application of means. There may be a miracle among its antecedent causes, or there may not. The apostles employed miracles simply as the means by which they arrested attention to their message and established its divine authority. But the miracle was not the revival.

I said that a revival is the result of the *right* use of the appropriate means. The means that God has enjoined for the production of a revival doubtless have a natural tendency to produce a revival. Otherwise God would not have enjoined them. But means will not produce a revival, we all know, without the blessing of God. It is impossible for us to say that there is not as direct an influence or agency from God to produce a crop of grain as there is to produce a revival.

I wish to impress this idea on your minds, for there has long been the prevalent thought that there is something peculiar about promoting Christianity, that it is not to be judged by the ordinary rules of cause and effect. No doctrine is more dangerous than this to the prosperity of the church and nothing more absurd.

Suppose a man were to preach this doctrine among farmers about their sowing grain. Suppose he tell the farmer that God is sovereign and will give him a crop only when it pleases Him, and that for him to plow and plant and labor as if he expected to raise a crop himself is very wrong and would be taking the work out of the hands of God, interfering with His sovereignty. And now suppose all farmers should believe such doctrine. The world would starve to death. The same result will follow if the church is persuaded that promoting the Christian faith is somehow so mysteriously a subject of divine sovereignty that there is no natural connection between the means and the end.

There is one fact under the government of God worthy of universal notice and of everlasting remembrance: The most useful and important things are most easily and certainly obtained by the use of the appropriate means. It is evident that this is a principle in the divine administration. Hence all the necessities of life are obtained with great certainty by the use of the simplest means. This principle holds true in moral government, as well. And because spiritual blessings are of surpassing importance, we should expect their attainment to be connected with the use of the appropriate means. I fully believe that were the facts fully known, it would be found that when the appointed means have been rightly used, spiritual blessings have been obtained with greater uniformity than temporal ones.

What a revival is

A revival consists of Christians being renewed in their first love, resulting in the awakening and conversion of sinners to God. In the popular sense, a revival of religion in a community is the awakening, quickening, and reclaiming of the backslidden church and the general awakening of all classes, insuring attention to the claims of God.

1. A revival always includes conviction of sin on the part of the church. Backslidden professors cannot wake up and begin again in the service of God without a deep searching of heart. The fountains of sin need to be broken up.

2. Backslidden Christians will be brought to repentance. A revival is nothing less than a new beginning of obedience to God,

including deep humility and forsaking of sin—just as in the case of a converted sinner the first step is deep repentance.

3. Christians will have their faith renewed. While they are in a backslidden state they are blind to the plight of sinners. Their hearts are as hard as marble. The truths of the Bible appear as a dream. They admit to its being true; their conscience and their reason assent to it; but their faith does not see it standing out in bold relief, in all the burning reality of eternity. But when they enter into revival, they no longer see men as trees walking; they see things in the strong light that renews the love of God in their hearts. This will lead them to labor zealously to bring others to Him.

4. A revival breaks the power of the world and of sin over Christians. It brings them to the point of receiving a fresh impulse toward heaven: they have a new foretaste of it, and a new desire for union with God; the charm of the world is broken and the power of sin is overcome.

5. When the churches are thus awakened and reformed, the salvation of sinners will follow, going through the same stages of conviction, repentance, and change.

So it is clear what revival is, but I fear we have not seen it on a large scale in our day because we have been waiting for God to do what is our responsibility to do. At Wheaton College we found the truth of 2 Chronicles 7:14: "If my people, who are called by my name, will humble themselves and pray and seek my face and turn from their wicked ways, then will I hear from heaven and will forgive their sin and will heal their land." It was our part to humble ourselves, to pray earnestly and expectantly, to seek the Lord, and to turn from all known sin. Then there came a gracious and mighty visitation from heaven. We then understood what Finney meant in his classic statement on the sovereignty of God and the use of means in revival, as is true in every aspect of the divine government:

Many people have supposed God's sovereignty to be something very different from what it is. They have supposed it to be such an arbitrary disposal of events, and particularly of the gift of His Spirit, as precluded a rational employment of means for promoting a revival of religion. But there is no evidence from the Bible that God exercises any such sovereignty. There are no facts to prove it. But everything goes to show that God has connected means with the end through all the departments of His government—in nature and in grace. There is no natural event in which His own agency is not concerned. He has not built creation like a vast machine that will go on alone without His further care. He has not retired from the universe to let it work for itself. This is mere atheism. He exercises a universal superintendence and control. And yet every event in nature has been brought about by means. He neither administers providence nor grace with that sort of sovereignty that dispenses with the use of means. There is no more sovereignty in one than in the other.

And yet some people are terribly alarmed at all direct efforts to promote a revival. They say things like, *You are trying to get up a revival in your own strength,* or *You are interfering with the sovereignty of God. Better to keep along the usual course, and let God give a revival when He thinks best,* or they say, *God is sovereign; it is wrong for you to attempt to get up a revival just because you think a revival is needed.* But this is just the kind of reasoning the devil wants. And men cannot do the devil's work more effectually than by preaching that the sovereignty of God is the reason why we should not put forth efforts to produce a revival.

Divine sovereignty designates devices and patterns for the procedure and success of divine purposes.

When Is Revival Needed?

In one sense, revival is needed constantly in the Christian church, for we always need the undiminished power of the Holy

Spirit; but in the usual sense of the term, revival is occasional rather than continual, and it is more desperately needed at some times than at others.

Finney faced the question, *When is a revival of religion needed in the churches and among Christians?* with his usual discernment, candor, and urgency. He maintained that such an awakening is indispensable when the following conditions prevail:

1. *A revival is needed when there is a lack of brotherly love and Christian camaraderie among professors of religion.* Then there comes a loud call for God to revive His work. When Christians have fallen into a backslidden state, they neither have nor ought to have, nor is there reason to have, the same love and confidence toward one another as when they are alert and active and living holy lives.

2. *When there is dissension and jealousy and evil speaking among professors of religion, there is a great need for revival.* These things show that Christians have gotten away from God and it is time to think earnestly of a revival. True Christian life cannot prosper with such things in the church, and nothing can put an end to them like a revival.

3. *When there is a worldly spirit in the church, when Christians begin to conform to the world in all manner of dress, language, and entertainment, there is need of a revival.*

4. *When the church finds its members succumbing to sin and decay, then it is time for the church to awake and cry to God for revival.* When such things are taking place as give the enemies of religion an occasion for reproach, it is time for the church to ask God, "What will come of thy great name?"

5. *When there is a spirit of controversy in the church or in the land, a revival is needful.* The spirit of Christ is not the spirit of controversy. There can be no prosperity in religion where the spirit of controversy prevails.

6. *When unbelievers revile the church and triumph over it, then it is time to seek for a true revival.*

7. *When Christians are careless of their actions and become*

unconcerned about their consequences, it is time for the church to stir itself to accountability and awaken to see the lost all around. Just as the fire fighter rouses in the night at the sound of an alarm and goes to rescue those who are trapped in the flames, so the church must revive itself to the sounds of danger and despair and rescue lost sinners from certain destruction.

———

Religious conditions in America at the turn of the nineteenth century were similar to what they are now at the dawn of the twenty-first—Christian accountability and spiritual life at low ebb. Skepticism and indifference were the result of English deism brought to the Colonies by British officers in the French and Indian Wars. Infidelity from the French revolutionists played a part, as well as the impact of two world wars within a generation (the Seven Years' War and the long struggle against France under revolutionists and Napoleon) and the impact of Europe's "Age of Reason." Then the Second Awakening swept across the Eastern Seaboard to the farthest frontier of Kentucky and Tennessee. The churches revived, schools prospered, national morality was lifted to a high level, and American destiny under God continued to move westward.

When we apply Finney's analysis of conditions that call for a return to God to the religious climate of our day, we see that revival is the greatest need of the hour. In addition, for our encouragement, he lists indications that show when a revival might be expected:

1. *When the providence of God indicates that a revival is at hand.* These indications are sometimes so plain as to amount to a revelation of His will. There will be a conspiring of events to open the way and a preparation of circumstances to favor the coming of a revival, so that those who are looking for it can see plainly that it is at hand.

2. *When the wickedness of sinners grieves, humbles, and distresses Christians.* Sometimes Christians do not seem to mind the

wickedness around them, or if they do talk about it, it is in a cold, callous, and unfeeling manner. But when the conduct of the wicked drives Christians to prayer, breaks them down, and makes them sorrowful and tenderhearted toward the offenders so that they weep for them instead of scolding and reproaching them, you may expect a revival.

3. *When Christians possess a true spirit of prayer for revival.* That is, when believers pray as if they expect a revival. Sometimes Christians are not inclined to pray at all for revival, and even when they do it in a perfunctory manner, their minds are somewhere else. They may be praying for the salvation of the heathen but not for revival among themselves. When they feel a true need for revival, they will pray for it earnestly—for their own families and neighborhoods—as if they would not be denied.

4. *When the attention of ministers is especially directed toward this particular subject.* When the messages of preachers as well as their other efforts are directed toward the spiritual state of the families in their congregation, and their hearts are full of passion for the coming of revival, you may expect one.

5. *When Christians begin to confess their sins to one another.* At other times, Christians may confess sins in a general manner, as if only half in earnest. They may do it in eloquent language but without sincerity. But when there is a spontaneous breaking down and a pouring out of the heart in making confession of sin, the floodgates will burst open and salvation will flow over the whole place.

6. *When Christians are willing to make the sacrifice necessary to see revival flourish and continue.* Christians must be willing to sacrifice their personal feelings, their business or work schedules, and their free time to help a revival move forward and complete its work. Ministers also must be willing to "lay down their lives" for the sake of revival.

7. *When ministers and layworkers are willing to have God promote revival by whatever instruments He pleases.* Sometimes ministers are not willing to have a revival unless *they* can have the

management of it or unless *their* agency can be conspicuous in promoting it. They wish to prescribe to God what He will direct and bless and what men He shall put to the forefront. But for revival to occur they must be willing to have anyone or anything employed that will do the most good.

8. *When the foregoing is all in place, a revival, in the strictest sense, already exists.* A revival should be *expected* whenever it is *needed*. If we need to be revived, we should be revived. We should expect it and work toward it as though it were inevitable.

A revival generally begins in a very small and inconspicuous place, and the fire spreads elsewhere as fanned by the breath of God. Jonathan Edwards noted that the awakening in eighteenth-century Massachusetts began "at a little village called Pascommuck, when only a few families were settled," and then caught fire in Northampton. Under Finney it began in a tiny rural community called Evans Mills. Often it comes simultaneously, or nearly so, in widely scattered places, and spreads to adjoining areas. It is as though the outer dry leaves of an autumn bonfire are kindled; then, as the inner leaves are dried by the heat and are stirred by a rake or pitchfork, they also burst into flame. The apparently incombustible leaves catch fire because of those already aflame.

Revival Preaching

"So is my word that goes out from my mouth: It will not return to me empty, but will accomplish what I desire and achieve the purpose for which I sent it." This was the word of the Lord through Isaiah (55:11), the evangelical prophet of the old dispensation. The fisherman preacher of the new era spoke warmly of those who "preached the gospel to you by the Holy Spirit sent from heaven" (1 Peter 1:12b). To be effective, revival preaching must be scriptural, sane, and earnest, yet fiery. While the contents of revival preaching vary but little from generation to generation, the manner of presentation is peculiar to each preacher and his era. Preaching should be the outpouring of the Spirit through the speaker, and the methods of preaching will vary with the personality of the messenger. The sermon may be sweet yet searching, quiet yet convincing, gentle as the dew from heaven or with torrents of emotion that sweep away all opposition and indifference in its path. Asahel Nettleton, an American evangelist, himself a product of the revivals at Yale under the scholarly and spiritually minded president Timothy Dwight, was widely used of God as a soul winner, and his preaching was unassuming, earnest, and unemotional, yet very effective. Peter Cartwright, a fiery Methodist evangelist and circuit rider on the Illinois frontier, was, at least as far as presentation, an exact opposite of Nettleton. Finney occupied a middle ground between the scholarly and searching Calvinistic evangelism of Nettleton and Cartwright's furious and fiery Arminianism. Finney was himself—as he should have been. From his *Lectures on Revival* and from his printed sermons we have much to learn about revival preaching used of God.

Two important factors in revival preaching are that it be *scriptural* and *doctrinal*. Nettleton and Finney were alike in that regard. Moody's preaching was empty until he became a man of the Book in the power of the Spirit. R. A. Torrey was as much a teacher of the Word as a preacher, and Billy Graham's messages, which have turned thousands to Christ, are biblical from beginning to end. Let an old divine, deeply taught in the Word and in revival experience, speak to the point. As pastor and later president of Princeton, Ashbel Green wrote from wide and deep experience:

> I would say briefly that in a time of revival, so far am I from thinking that the preaching employed should be merely exhortatory and principally addressed to the feelings, that I am persuaded it ought to be eminently doctrinal. Lively and tender and close and full of application it certainly should be; but the great and fundamental doctrines of the gospel should be brought out clearly—be lucidly explained and much insisted on. There ought to be a good many of what I would call

discriminating discourses—in which true religion should be distinguished from every counterfeit and the danger of embracing and resting on a false hope be fully exhibited. Of what may be denominated by way of eminence, gospel preaching ought not to lack; that is, the all-sufficiency of the Lord Jesus Christ to save even the chief of sinners, and His readiness to receive them when they come to Him in the exercise of faith and a contrite spirit—His readiness to cleanse them in His atoning blood, to clothe them with His perfect righteousness, to justify them freely, to sanctify them by His Spirit, to adopt them into His family, and to crown them with eternal glory, should be set forth in the most clear and persuasive manner. The true nature of regeneration—of evangelical faith, genuine repentance, and new obedience—should be carefully explained and illustrated. The danger of grieving away the Spirit of grace by those with whom He is striving, and the danger of all *delay* in accepting the gospel offer, should be often brought into view. The peril to the unawakened and the careless, when others are anxious and pressing into the kingdom of God—the awful peril of passing a season of revival without sharing in its blessed effects should often be pressed home on those who remain at ease in their sins. . . .

Finney, from his long and Spirit-filled service, made extended comment on revival preaching. He said that the Scriptures ascribe the conversion of a sinner to four different agencies—to *men*, to *God*, to the *truth*, and to the *sinner himself*. The passages that ascribe it to the truth are the largest class. That men should ever have overlooked this distinction and should have regarded conversion as a work performed exclusively by God is surprising.

The Bible speaks on this subject precisely as we speak on common subjects. If there is a man who has been very sick, it is natural for him to say of his physician, "That man saved my life." Does it mean to say that the physician saved his life without reference to God? Certainly not, unless the patient is an infidel. God made the physician, and he made the medicine, too. And it never can be shown but that the agency of God is just as truly concerned in making the medicine take effect to save a life as it is in making the truth take effect to save a soul. To affirm the contrary is downright atheism. It is true, then, that the physician saved him, but it is also true that God saved him. It is equally true that the medicine saved his life and that he saved his own life by taking the medicine; for the medicine would have done no good if he had not voluntarily taken it or yielded his body to its power.

In the conversion of a sinner, it is true that God gives the truth the capacity to turn the sinner to God. God is an active, voluntary, powerful agent in changing the mind. But He is not the only agent. The one that brings the truth to the sinner's notice is also an agent. We are apt to speak of ministers and other men as only *instruments* in converting sinners. This is not exactly correct. Man is something more than an instrument. Truth is the mere unconscious instrument. But man is the more responsible agent in the business because his help is voluntary.

Suppose yourself to be standing on the banks of Niagara Falls. As you are within view of the precipice, you notice a man lost in deep reverie, approaching its edge unconscious of his danger. He glides nearer and nearer in his small craft until he is within feet of the drop-off. At this moment you lift your voice in warning above the roar of the foaming waters, and cry out, "Stop!" The voice pierces his ear and breaks the charm that binds him; he dips his oar and turns his boat just in time to avoid disaster. All pale and aghast, he retires on the shore, and says, "That man saved my life!" He ascribes the saving work to you; and certainly there is a sense in which you have saved him. But upon further questioning, he says, "*Stop!* How that word rings in my ears. It was to me the word of life!" Now he ascribes his rescue to the *word* that reached him and caused him to turn. On conversing still further, he says, "Had I not turned at that instant, I would have been a dead man." Here he speaks of his own action; but then you hear him exclaim, "Oh, the mercy of God! If God had not interposed, I would have been lost."

Now, the only defect in this illustration is this: in the case supposed, the only interference on the part of God was a *providential* one; and the only sense in which the saving of the man's life is ascribed to Him is in a providential sense. But in the conversion of a sinner there is something more than the providence of God employed, for here not only does the providence of God so order it that the preacher cries *Stop!* but the Spirit of God also urges the truth home upon the sinner with such tremendous power as to induce him to turn.

Important particulars growing out of this subject as it is connected with preaching the gospel, and which show that great practical wisdom is indispensable to the winning of souls to Christ are:

1. *All preaching should be practical.* The proper end of all doctrine is practice. Anything promoted as doctrine that cannot be made use of as practical is not preaching the gospel.

"All Scripture is God-breathed and is useful for teaching, rebuking, correcting and training in righteousness, so that the man of God may be thoroughly equipped for every good work" (2 Timothy 3:16–17). A vast deal of preaching in the present day, as well as in past ages, is called *doctrinal* as opposed to *practical* preaching. The very idea of making this distinction is a device of the devil. To preach doctrines in an abstract way and not in reference to practice is absurd. The very design of doctrine is to regulate practice. To bring out doctrinal views for any other purpose is not only nonsense, it is wicked.

Some people are opposed to *doctrinal* preaching. If they have been used to hearing doctrine preached in a cold, abstract way, it is no wonder they are opposed to it. They ought to be opposed to such preaching. But what can a man preach if he does not preach doctrine? If he preaches no doctrine, he preaches no gospel. But if he does not preach it in a practical way, he hinders the gospel. A loose, exhortatory style of preaching may affect the emotions and may produce enthusiasm, but it will never sufficiently instruct people to secure a sound conversion.

2. *All preaching should be direct.* The gospel should be

preached *to* men and women and not *about* them. The minister must address his hearers. He must preach *to* them *about themselves* and not leave the impression that he is preaching to them about others. He will never do anyone any more good than his success at convincing each individual that he is preaching to that individual. Many preachers are reluctant to give the impression that they are preaching to individuals in particular. They preach against certain *sins* but do not relate them to the *sinner*. It is the *sin*, not the *sinner*, that they are rebuking, they say, and they would by no means speak as if they supposed any of *their hearers* were guilty of these abominable practices. Now, this is anything but preaching the gospel. Neither the prophets, nor the apostles, nor Christ himself preached without addressing the individual. Those ministers who preach in the abstract about sin are not successful in winning souls to Christ.

3. *Ministers should seek out sinners and Christians wherever they may have entrenched themselves in inaction.* It is not the design of preaching to make men comfortable and at rest but to make them *act*. A minister ought to know the religious opinions and views of every sinner in his congregation. Indeed, a minister in a small country church is generally inexcusable if he does not. Otherwise how can he preach to them? How can he effectively adapt the truth to their situation? How can he search them out unless he knows behind which sins they hide?

4. *A minister should spend the most time preaching on those particular points that are most needed.* For instance, he may have a group of people in his congregation who place great reliance on their own conclusions. They imagine that they can act at their own convenience and repent when they get ready, without any concern for the Spirit of God. The minister must show that this idea is contrary to the Scriptures—that if the Spirit of God is grieved away, however able the sinner may be, it is possible that he will never come to repentance, because when it is convenient for him to do so, he will have no such inclination. Others may hold views of election and sovereignty that cause them to think

they have nothing to do but wait for the moving of the Spirit. The minister must press home the fact of the sinner's ability to obey God and show him his obligation and duty to do so until he is saved. Wherever a sinner is entrenched, unless you pour light upon him there, you will never move him.

I have been in many places in times of revival, and I have never been able to employ precisely the same course of preaching in one place as in another. Some hearers are settled behind one refuge and some behind another. In one place, the *church* will need to be instructed; in another, *sinners*. In one place, one set of truths; in another, another set. A minister must find out where the people stand and preach accordingly. I believe this is the experience of all preachers who are called to labor from field to field.

5. *A minister must be very careful not to introduce controversy.* He will grieve away the Spirit of God if he does. Probably more revivals are put down in this way than in any other. Look back upon the history of the church from the beginning, and you will see that ministers are generally responsible for grieving away the Spirit and causing regression by controversy. It is usually the ministers who bring up controversial subjects for discussion and become very zealous about them. In this way the church takes on a controversial spirit, and the Spirit of God is grieved away. If in preaching a minister finds it necessary to discuss particular points about which Christians differ in opinion, let him *by all means* avoid a controversial spirit and manner of doing it.

6. *Messages should be preached in such a way that the whole gospel is brought before the minds of the people so as to produce its proper influence.* If too much stress is laid on one narrow subject, others will not have their proper portion. The symmetry of the message or series of messages will be unbalanced. If a subject is almost exclusively dwelt upon that requires great exertion of mind before it is understood by the heart and the conscience, the church will be indoctrinated in that narrow view and will have their heads filled without being awake, active, and efficient in the promotion of true Christianity. If, on the other hand, the preach-

ing is loose, indefinite, exhortatory, and highly impassioned, the church will be like a ship with too much sail for her ballast. It will be in danger of being swept away by a tempest of feeling where there is not sufficient knowledge to prevent their being carried away with every wind of doctrine.

7. *A sinner should be made to feel his guilt and not be left with the impression that he is merely unfortunate.* I think this is a very common fault, particularly with books published on the subject. They are calculated to make the sinner think more of his problems than of his sins and to feel that his state is *unfortunate* rather than in *opposition* to God.

8. *The obligation to act now must be emphasized.* I have talked with thousands of convicted sinners and found that the majority had never before felt the Spirit's urging to repent as they were presently feeling. But, unfortunately, the fact that sinners are expected to repent when they feel the conviction of the Holy Spirit is not the impression that is commonly made by ministers in their preaching. If they suppose that they are making this impression, they are deceived. Most commonly, almost any other idea but that they are expected to repent now and not later is made upon the minds of sinners.

9. *Sinners ought to be made to feel that they have something to do and that it is something no one else can do for them.* Neither God nor man can repent for another man. Finding salvation is something to *do* and not something to *wait for*. Repentance is something they must do *now*, or they put themselves in danger of being eternally lost.

10. *Ministers should not rest until they have annihilated every excuse of sinners.* The plea of "inability" is the worst of all excuses. It slanders God, charging Him with infinite tyranny in commanding men to do what they have no power to do. The sinner should be made to see and feel that this is the very nature of his excuse. He must see that all pleas for not submitting to God are acts of rebellion against Him. Take away the last lie that he holds to and

let him know that without repentance he is absolutely condemned before God.

11. *Sinners should be made aware that if they grieve away the Spirit of God now, it is possible that they will be lost forever.* There is infinite danger of this. They should be made to understand *why* they are dependent on the Spirit, and that it is not because they *cannot* do what God commands but because they are *unwilling* to do it. Show them, too, the common fact that most who hear the gospel and are converted experience this at a young age. The tendency is to put it off with the idea that they will decide at a later date—when they are older. When the truth is preached, sinners become either gospel-hardened or converted. Some are converted when they are older, but this is the exception, not the rule.

Preaching on the subject of hell is usually common in revivals, but is always bitterly criticized by the unsaved and the indifferent. The awful truth of an eternity separated from God for the impenitent and unbelieving is declared in the Scriptures from beginning to end. No heart was ever more tender than that of the Lord Jesus, and yet no one ever spoke more authoritatively or earnestly on the reality of hell than He did. His many warnings include: "Do not be afraid of those who kill the body but cannot kill the soul. Rather, be afraid of the One who can destroy both soul and body in hell" (Matthew 10:28); "The Son of man will send out his angels, and they will weed out of his kingdom everything that causes sin and all who do evil. They will throw them into the fiery furnace, where there will be weeping and gnashing of teeth" (Matthew 13:41–42); "What good will it be for a man if he gains the whole world, yet forfeits his own soul?" (Matthew 16:26); "It is better for you to enter life maimed or crippled than to have two hands or two feet and be thrown into eternal fire" (Matthew 18:8).

Jonathan Edwards defended in his day the use of strong and impassioned preaching to the awakened as well as to the indifferent by comparing the preacher who preaches the truth without comfort to the surgeon who does what is necessary for the body even when the patient complains that he doesn't want to undergo surgery. No conscientious surgeon would tell his patient he could forego a necessary surgery even though it will save his life, simply because the patient fears it or feels it is unnecessary. It would be like crying, "Peace, peace," when there is no peace.

Finney preached pointedly, earnestly, and effectively on the issues of eternity. A careful study of his burning message on "Moral Insanity" will show how deeply he felt on the matter and how clearly he presented the truth of the awful "madhouse of the universe," where the spiritually insane, however intellectually sane they may have been, will be institutionalized forever.

The preaching that in the power of the Spirit produces revival is practical, pointed, personal, pungent, and in proper proportions. Stress should be made on not neglecting to preach truths that are seldom covered, for it seems that the Spirit of God uses in a particular manner the gospel message that is unfamiliar. In the day of Edwards and Whitefield, it was the preaching of the new birth that stirred multitudes to their need of the Savior. In the Second Awakening, Timothy Dwight fought unbelief by all his powers of logic and exhortation, until Yale students began to realize they were lost sinners and not smug philosophers. Finney preached human responsibility and ability in a generation of hyper-Calvinism and Universalism.

What areas of scriptural truth have we neglected that when preached will produce revival?

The Pew and the Pulpit

The most powerful preaching in the world will never produce revival as long as there remains inconsistency or indifference on the part of Christian people. If Christians are careless and carefree, why should sinners be concerned? The church that is cold and thoughtless about eternal values, with concern almost entirely for the passing pleasures and treasures of this world, creates a false comfort for the unsaved. Finney observed that among such church members, their very manner of conversation upon leaving the sanctuary contradicted the sermon. When this was the case, he cautioned, "the minister may warn every man daily with tears and it will produce no effect."

Where the church testifies against the gospel by a careless life, sinners will be "gospel-hardened"; but once the Christians begin to wake up, to search out their own hearts, to begin to obey the Lord and to live lives consistent with their faith, then the sinner will begin to feel his need. Finney learned by experience that if the church lived only one week as if they truly believed the Bible, sinners would fall down before them and ask how they might be saved. In challenging Christians to consistency of life, he declared, "Every step you take, you tread on chords that will vibrate to all eternity. Every time you move, you touch keys whose sound will echo through the hills and dales of heaven and through the dark corners and vaults of hell. Every moment of your lives you are exerting a tremendous influence that will tell on the immortal interests of souls all around you. Are you asleep while your conduct is exerting such an influence?"

How then is the Christian in the pew to corroborate the preacher in the pulpit? Finney made pertinent and pointed reply:

> By precept and example—on every proper occasion by their lips but mainly by their lives. Christians have no right to be silent: they should rebuke, exhort, and entreat with all long-suffering and doctrine. But their main influence as witnesses is by their example. They are required to be witnesses in this way, because example teaches with so much greater force than precept. This is universally known. Actions speak louder than words. They should live in their daily walk and conversation as if they believed the Bible with all their hearts.

1. *Christians should live as if they believed the soul to be immortal, and as if they believed that death were not the termination of their existence but the entrance into an unchanging state.* They ought to live so as to make this distinct impression upon all those around them.

2. *They are to testify by their life the vanity and unsatisfying nature of the things of this world*. Failure in this is the great stumbling block in the way of humankind. Here the testimony of God's children is needed more than anywhere else. People are so taken up with tangible objects, so constantly occupied with them, that they are very apt to shut out eternity from their minds.

3. *Christians are bound to show by their conduct that they are actually satisfied with the joys of their faith—without the pomp and vanity of the world; that the pleasure of communion with God keeps them unaffected by the things of this world*. They are to manifest that this world is not their home, that heaven is a reality, and that they expect to dwell there forever.

4. *They must warn sinners of their fearful condition and exhort them to flee from the wrath to come*, to lay hold on everlasting life. But who does not know that the *manner* in which this is done is everything? Sinners are often brought under conviction by the very manner in which they are approached. By way of illustration, there was a man who was very much opposed to a certain preacher. On being asked to specify some reason, he replied, "I can't bear to hear him, for he says the word *hell* in such a way that it rings in my ears for a long time afterward." On the contrary, if a woman were to tell her unconverted husband in a casual, joking manner, "My dear, I believe you are going to hell," it is not likely that he will take her seriously.

5. *The Christian must bear witness to the reality of the love of Christ by the regard that is shown for His precepts, His honor, and His kingdom*. He must behave as if he truly believes that Christ died for the sins of the whole world. This is the only way to impress sinners with the love of Christ. Unfortunately, Christians often live so as to give the impression that Christ is so compassionate that sinners have very little to fear.

6. *They must realize the necessity of holiness in order to enter heaven*. It will not do to simply talk about this. We must live holy lives, not presumptuously but in confidence that we have the ho-

liness of Christ when we have appropriated His sacrifice and live in obedience to Him.

7. *Christians ought to show by their own example the necessity of self-denial, humility, and spiritual-mindedness.* This is the most powerful preaching, after all, and the most likely to have an influence on the impenitent—by showing them the great difference between the sinner and the Christian.

8. *The people of God ought always to display a temperament like that of the Son of God—meek, unassuming, unselfish—who when He was reviled, reviled not again.* Nothing makes so solemn an impression upon sinners and bears down upon the conscience with such force as to see a Christian who is truly Christlike—bearing affronts and injuries with the meekness of a lamb. It cuts like a two-edged sword.

9. *The Christian must be entirely honest without exception in all avenues of life.* The Christian should show the strictest regard to integrity in every business decision and activity and in all relations with his fellowmen. If every Christian would pay scrupulous attention to honesty and always be conscientious to do the right thing, it would make a powerful impression on people's minds of the reality of Christian principle.

Only as the Christian in the pew substantiates by word and life the preacher in the pulpit will gospel preaching produce revival.

Personal Witnessing

"He that wins souls is wise," said the wisest of men in Old Testament times. "Follow me, and I will make you fishers of men," declared the Savior, as He called the first disciples to His service. Fish are not caught by careless or listless fishermen who make no study of the haunts and habits of these creatures of the deep, and neither are souls won to the Savior by witnesses who are uninstructed or disinterested. Soul winning is the greatest occupation in the world, the most satisfying and the most rewarding. Daniel declared, "Those who are wise will shine like the brightness of the heavens, and those who lead many to righteousness, like the stars for ever and ever" (12:3).

Finney was a master fisherman, and from his wide and effectual experience he gives us helpful information on how to deal with sinners, both those who are careless and indifferent and those who are awakened but unsaved.

The manner of dealing with careless sinners

Timing is all-important in making a serious impression on the mind of a careless sinner. If the time is not right, you will likely fail to make any impression at all. You may argue that it is our duty at all times to warn sinners and to awaken them to their need. But I contend that unless advantage is taken of the proper time, they will not hear you.

1. *It is most desirable, if possible, to address a person that is careless about his soul when he is disengaged from other occupations*. If his attention is taken up with something else, it will be very difficult to awaken him to his spiritual need. People who are careless and indifferent toward religion are often offended rather than benefited by being called away from other important business.

2. *It is also important to talk with a person about his soul when he is not preoccupied with any other subject*. If he is concerned at the moment about something else, he will not be in any frame of mind to be addressed on the subject of religion.

3. *Be sure that the person you speak with is perfectly sober and in a quiet, restful state*. To approach a person who is intoxicated or otherwise hindered as to his normal capacity for comprehension is to waste time and words.

4. *If possible, talk to someone about his salvation when he is in a generally good mood*. If you find him out of humor, very probably he will only become angry or try to argue with you. Better to leave him alone and not quench the Spirit. You may think you can talk him into a good mood, but it is not likely.

5. *When possible, take the opportunity to converse with a person careless of his soul when he is alone.* Most people are too proud to be in conversation about their spiritual needs in the presence of others, even family members. In public, a man will bristle and proudly defend himself, while when alone, he might quietly receive the truth.

6. *Seize the opportunity to talk with someone about his soul when the power of the Spirit or providential circumstances are in your favor.* If a particular event should occur, for example, which would certainly enhance the subject to be broached, try to take advantage of the situation in a positive way.

7. *Take the earliest opportunity to engage in conversation with those around you who are without faith.* Do not put it off from day to day, hoping for a more convenient situation.

8. *If you have strong feelings about witnessing to a particular individual, take the first opportunity to talk with that one while your strong inclination persists.* Your feelings are likely an indication of the moving of the Spirit of God.

Further suggestions with regard to the manner of witnessing

1. *When you approach an individual in an effort to awaken him to his soul's condition, be sure to treat him kindly.* Let him see that you are not seeking a quarrel with him but that you love his soul and desire his best good for now and eternity.

2. *Be serious. Avoid levity in your manner and language.* You are, after all, engaged in a very solemn work that will affect the character of your friend or neighbor and maybe even determine his destiny for eternity.

3. *Be respectful.* Some seem to think it is necessary to be abrupt, rude, or coarse in their conversation with the worldly and impenitent. Nothing could be further from the truth. The apostle Paul has given us a better rule: "Make sure that nobody pays back wrong for wrong, but always try to be kind to each other and to everyone else" (1 Thessalonians 5:15).

4. *Be sure to be very plain and straightforward*. Do not try to cover up or ignore facts of the person's character or his relationship to God. Lay it out in the open, not for the purpose of offending or wounding him, but because it is necessary to the healing and restoration process. Do not hold back the truth, but allow it to do its work.

5. *Address the conscience of the individual*. In a sermon, ministers can probe the emotions of their audience and thus awaken the mind. But in private conversation you cannot pour out the truth in the same impassioned manner. And unless you address the conscience pointedly, you will not reach the mind at all.

6. *Stress the great and fundamental truths of Scripture*. Unbelievers are apt to go off on some pretext or subordinate point, especially one of sectarianism. Make it clear that the first priority is to save his soul, not settle controversial theological questions. Hold him to the truths by which he must be saved or lost.

7. *Be very patient*. If your hearer has some difficulty in his mind with regard to doctrine or disparity among believers, be very patient until you find out what it is, and then seek to clear it up. Do not try to answer him by argument, but rather show that his question is not pertinent to his salvation.

8. *Take care to guard your own spirit*. There are many who do not have the patience and calm to converse with someone who is opposed to Christianity. And a person in serious opposition wants nothing more than to see you angry. He will go away in triumph if he has succeeded in reviling you.

9. *If the sinner is inclined to hold out against God, be careful not to take his side in anything*. Sometimes a cynical unbeliever will seek to find fault with Christians or with God. Do not take his side against your brothers or try to defend God; He will defend himself. Simply tell him he does not have to answer for the sins of others, only for his own.

10. *Bring up particular sins of the individual of which you are aware*. Talking in general terms against sin will produce no result.

You must make the person feel that the gospel concerns him in particular.

11. *It is generally best to be concise and to the point and not draw out what you have to say.* Get the person's attention as soon as you can to the point of the gospel and then press him to have at least an opinion on it. If it seems the Spirit is moving the person, ask if he would like to repent and receive Christ. This is the real issue. Carefully avoid making the impression that nothing has to be done *now*.

12. *Be sure to pray with the individual, regardless of whether he is ready to receive Christ.* It is important to commit the matter to God and to show that all things are best concluded with prayer. Any evangelical work that does not include prayer is an unfinished work.

The manner of dealing with awakened sinners

Be careful to distinguish between an awakened sinner and one who is under serious conviction of sin. When you speak with a person who has some feelings on the subject of Christianity, do not take for granted that he is under conviction of sin. Persons are often merely awakened by some providential circumstance—sickness, natural disaster, accident, severe disappointment, or a death in the family. Perhaps the Spirit of God has opened their minds and hearts to the seriousness of life and they are ready to hear the gospel. If you find a person awakened, no matter by what means, lose no time in pouring light into his mind. Once you have a sinner's attention, very often his conviction and even conversion is the work of a few moments. You can sometimes do more in five minutes with a person who is enlightened and interested than you could do in years while the person is careless about his soul or indifferent to the gospel.

I have been amazed at the lack of discernment on the part of parents who will allow a child awakened to his sin to remain in that state for days and weeks and not say a word to him on the subject of faith. They say that if the Spirit of God has begun a work in him, He will certainly carry it through. On the contrary, such a child ought to be spoken to immediately, as soon as he is awakened, and the light of the truth be poured into his mind without delay. If that favorable moment is lost, it may never be recovered.

I have often seen Christians in revivals who were constantly on the lookout to see if anyone appeared to be awakened to their spiritual need. And as soon as they saw anyone begin to manifest emotion under the power of the preaching of the Word, they would approach him as soon as the meeting was over, invite him to a room alone, and converse and pray with him, and if possible not leave him until he was converted.

The manner of dealing with "convicted" sinners

By a *convicted* sinner, I mean one who feels condemned by the law of God as truly guilty of sin. He has had enough instruction to understand something of the extent of God's law and he sees and feels his guilt and may even know what the remedy is. To deal with these persons requires great wisdom.

1. *When a person is convicted and not converted, but remains in an anxious state about his soul, there is generally some specific reason for it.* In such cases, it does no good to exhort him to repent or to explain the law to him. He knows all that; he understands all the general points. But still he does not repent. There must be some particular difficulty to overcome. You may preach and pray and exhort till doomsday and not gain anything.

You must then determine to find out what the particular difficulty is. A physician who examines a patient and finds him sick with a particular disease, first administers the general remedies that are applicable. If these produce no effect, and the disease continues unabated, he must examine the individual case and learn the constitution of the patient—his habits, his diet, his manner of living, to see why the medicine does not take effect. So it is with the case of a sinner convicted but not converted. If ordinary instructions and exhortations fail, there must be some difficulty involved. Often it is known to the individual, though he may conceal it. Sometimes it is something that has escaped his observation.

(a) The individual may have some idol, something that he loves more than God and which prevents him from giving himself up entirely to God. You must find out what it is that he will not give up, as a means of helping him.

(b) Perhaps he has injured another individual and he is unwilling to confess it or to make a proper recompense. Inform him that until he is willing to confess and forsake this sin, he will find no mercy.

(c) Sometimes there is a particular sin that he will not forsake. He tells himself it is only a small one or tries to persuade himself it is not a sin at all. He must be made to understand that all sin is serious and must be dealt with no matter how small it is.

(d) Perhaps there is some work of remuneration that he must do. Perhaps he has defrauded someone in business or taken some unfair advantage—contrary to the golden rule of doing as you would be done by—and is unwilling to make it right.

(e) He may be bound up by something and has convinced himself with regard to some particular point on which he is determined not to yield. Individuals are sometimes adamant that they will not go to a particular meeting—whether an inquiry meeting or a prayer meeting—or they will not have a certain person pray with them; or they will not take a particular seat, such as the anxious seat. They say that they can be converted without yielding on this point, for true faith does not consist in these things. This may be, but by taking this ground they *make* it the material point. And so long as they are stuck there and determined to bring God to their terms, they can never be converted. They will often yield anything else and do anything in the world but that one thing—which amounts to taking a stand against God. They cannot be humbled until they yield on this point, whatever it is.

(f) Perhaps he is prejudiced against someone, such as a member of the church. It may be on account of some faithful dealing with his soul, or something in his business that he did not like, and he hangs onto this, and will never be converted till he gives it up.

(g) He may feel ill will toward someone or be angry and cherish strong feelings of resentment that prevent him from obtaining mercy from God. "For if you forgive men when they sin against you, your heavenly Father will also forgive you. But if you do not forgive men their sins, your Father will not forgive your sins" (Matthew 6:14).

(h) Perhaps he entertains some error in doctrine or some wrong notion about how something is done that may be keeping him out of the kingdom. Perhaps he is waiting for God. He is convinced that he deserves to go to hell and that unless he is converted he will go there, but he is waiting for God to do something before he submits. He is, in fact, waiting for God to do for him what God has required that he do for himself. He may be waiting for more conviction. People often do not know what conviction is and think they are not under conviction, when, in fact, they are under powerful conviction.

Sometimes such people think their *sins are too great* to be forgiven or that they have grieved the Spirit of God away, when it is the Spirit who is convicting them. They contend that their sins are greater than Christ's mercies, which is actually an insult to His saving power.

Others go a step further with the idea that they are "given up" by God and cannot be saved. It is often very difficult to convince such persons otherwise. Many of the most distressing cases I have ever met with have been of this nature—persons who insisted that God had given up on them, and therefore they could not change.

Another angle on this excuse is that persons will strenuously maintain that they have committed the unpardonable sin. When they get that idea into their heads, they will turn everything you say against them. It is common for persons in such cases to keep their eyes only on themselves and their own darkness, rather than on Christ. Now, if you can get them to take their minds off themselves and to think of Christ's power and mercy, you may draw them away from brooding over their own feelings and failings and get them to lay hold on the hope set before them in the gospel.

2. *Be careful in conversing with convicted sinners not to make any compromise with them on any point where they have a difficulty*. If you do, they will be sure to take advantage of it and thus secure a false hope. Convicted sinners often get into a bind with regard to giving up some secret sin or yielding on some point where conscience and the Holy Spirit are at war. If they come across an individual who will yield the point, they feel better and are happy and even think they are converted. People are often amazingly anxious to make a compromise. They will ask questions like whether or not you think a person may be a Christian and yet do such and such a thing. Do not yield an inch on any such inquiry. You may be able to discern the very point they are laboring in their minds. They will often reveal to you unawares that it is pride or love of the world or something they cannot give up that prevents their becoming a Christian.

Be careful to cover thoroughly the point of the love of the world. I believe there have been more false hopes built on wrong instruction here than on any other point. The church is filled with hypocrites who have never given up the world. Many think they can be Christians and yet use all their time and money and property for their own ends and their own enjoyment, only giving a little now and then to save appearances and when they can do it with total convenience. But it is a sad mistake.

In dealing with a convicted sinner, be sure to steer him away from every refuge and not leave him an inch of ground to stand on so long as he resists God. This need not take a long time. When the Spirit of God is at work striving with a sinner, it is easy to lead him away from his refuges. You will find the truth to be like a hammer, crushing wherever it strikes. In a true conversion the person will give up everything for God.

5

The Price of Revival

As we have seen, revival is the coming of the inexpressibly sweet and tender Spirit of God into the midst of His people with convicting and transforming power. The outpouring of God's Spirit is the divine aspect of revival, while the preparation of the heart is our part. Many of the promises of God given in the Scriptures are made conditional upon our preparation of heart to receive them or our lack of preparation. The psalmist said plainly, "If I regard iniquity in my heart, the Lord will not hear me." The Lord Jesus said in teaching His disciples to have the faith of God, "For if you forgive men when they sin against you, your heavenly Father will also forgive you." John, who had been transformed from "Boanerges"—hot-tempered "son of thunder"—to the disciple of love, taught all his long life as he had been taught: "If we walk in the light, as he is in the light, we have fellowship with one another, and the blood of Jesus, his Son, purifies us from all sin. . . . If we confess our sins, he is faithful and just and will forgive us our sins and purify us from all unrighteousness." Forgiveness—*if*, cleansing from sin—*if*, fellowship—*if*. In the fulfillment of those gracious promises we have our part, and when we have done that, God is faithful to do His part.

One of the most familiar promises in the Word, more familiar perhaps to us in theory than in practice, is 2 Chronicles 7:14, wherein we have presented graphically and unequivocally the *price* of revival: "If my people, who are called by my name, will humble themselves and pray and seek my face and turn from their wicked ways, then will I hear from heaven and will forgive their sin and will heal their land."

One of the first lessons to be learned in revival is that it is extremely important to take *time* to have our inner ear tuned to the voice of God's Spirit, to have our hearts melted by His indwelling presence, to be willing to face ourselves and our sin, and to turn from it. Then we begin to understand why God's people in times of revival have lingered long in the presence of God and that neither time nor place seemed of any importance in the light of eternity and heaven. We can then understand how the remnant of Israel that had returned to Jerusalem under Ezra could sit "in the street of the house of God, trembling because of this matter, and for the great rain." The people had come to tenderness of heart because of their transgressions, and Ezra their leader prayed, "Give us a reviving, to set up the house of our God, and to repair the desolation thereof. . . . O Lord God of Israel, thou art righteous . . . behold, we are before thee in our trespasses."

When the Holy Spirit came to us at Wheaton College, we could well understand why the people in Nehemiah's day stood "from daybreak till noon" as the Word of God was read, and why, because of that word, "all the people were weeping," and why, on a later occasion, "those of Israelite descent had separated themselves from all foreigners. They stood in their places and confessed their sins and the wickedness of their fathers. They stood where they were and read from the Book of the Law of the LORD their God for a quarter of the day, and spent another quarter in confession and in worshiping the LORD their God" (8:2–9:3).

Jonathan Edwards, in the wisdom and grace given to him, made observation of the same factor, stating that we need "the exercise of great patience in *waiting on God*":

> And because such an extraordinary time as this especially requires of us the exercise of a great deal of forbearance toward one another, so there is peculiarly requisite in God's people the exercise of great patience in waiting on God in the face of any special difficulties and disadvantages that they may be under as to the means of grace. The beginning of a revival of religion will naturally and necessarily be attended with a great many difficulties of nature; many parts of the reviving church will, for a while, be under great disadvantages by reason of what remains of the old disease, of a general corruption of the visible church. We cannot expect that after a long time of degeneracy and depravity in the state of things in the church everything should come to rights all at once; it must be a work of time: and for God's people to be overhasty... in such a case, being resolved to have everything rectified at once, or else forcibly to deliver themselves by breaches and separations, is the way to hinder things coming to rights as they otherwise would and to keep them back....

Finney knew what it meant to have the Spirit of God come into a meeting with deep searching of heart for Christians and deep dismay for sinners, and that under such circumstances to dismiss the meeting was to destroy it and to dissipate the convicting, soul-healing power of the Spirit. Like Edwards before him, Finney was subjected to strong criticism because of "protracted meetings"; but the heart that knows the moving of God's Spirit in human hearts has no apprehension of the caustic criticism given by those who were not at the service or who were in opposition to it.

As was to be expected, we at Wheaton College were sharply criticized by some because of a service that lasted all Wednesday night, all day Thursday and Thursday night, and on into Friday. The *New York Times* of February 12, 1950, reporting on reactions to the revival, gave opinions of delegates at a denominational conference in Columbus, Ohio. Some religious leaders were willing to see what came of the awakening, but "one delegate, who asked that his name not be used, sharply criticized the president of the college for permitting the demonstration to continue so long. Charging the college head with a 'poor understanding of youthful adolescence,' he pointed out that under 'normal' circumstances and faced with a similar predicament, a trained religious educator would propose that the students continue their 'confessions' in private and 'honest' prayer."

The only answer to such criticism is that if the critic also had been with us in God's presence, I am sure he also would have sensed the solemnity and awe of the divine presence and his need of waiting on God. He would have learned, as we did, to understand what Andrew Murray says to us in his *Secret of Adoration*:

> Take time. Give God time to reveal himself to you. Give yourself time to be silent and quiet before Him, waiting to receive, through the Spirit, the assurance of His presence with you, His power working in you. Take time to read His Word as in His presence, that from it you may know what He asks of you and what He promises you. Let the Word create around you, create within you a holy atmosphere, a holy heavenly light, in which your soul will be refreshed and strengthened for the work of daily life.

If We Humble Ourselves . . .

To sit patiently and quietly in God's presence is to come to know one's own heart. When that is accomplished, we know what it is to humble ourselves before Him. We learn that the true secret of revival is Christians getting right with God, whatever may be the cost to them. Then it is not difficult to understand what Jonathan Edwards meant when he said:

> We ought to set ourselves about in the first place to remove stumbling blocks . . . and in order to do this there must be a great deal done at confessing of fault, on both sides, for un-

110

doubtedly many and great are the faults that have been committed in the conflicts and confusions, and mixtures of light
and darkness, that have been of late. There is hardly any duty
more contrary to our corrupt dispositions and mortifying to
the pride of man, but it must be done. Repentance of fault is,
in a peculiar manner, a proper duty when the kingdom of
heaven is at hand or when we especially expect or desire that
it should come, as appears by John the Baptist's preaching.
And if God does now loudly call upon us to repent, then he
also calls upon us to make proper manifestation of our repentance.

The confession of wrong is to be as private or public as the
committing of the sin. If we have wronged someone in thought,
the confession should be in the quiet of our own heart to the
Lord; on the other hand, if we have done injury to someone or to
the group, our confession should be also to them. Edwards continues his word about confessions:

> And on the other side, if those who have been zealous to
> promote the work have in any of the aforementioned instances
> openly gone much out of the way and done that which is con-
> trary to Christian rules, whereby they have openly injured oth-
> ers or greatly violated good order, and so done that which has
> wounded religion, they must publicly confess it, and humble
> themselves, as they would gather out the stones and prepare
> the way of God's people. They who have laid great stumbling
> blocks in others' way by *open transgression* are bound to re-
> move them by their *open repentance*.

The penitent and obedient heart then comes to know the reality of Proverbs 28:13: "He that conceals his sins does not prosper,
but whoever confesses and renounces them finds mercy."

To make urgent and emphatic this absolute essential of revival—the humbling of ourselves in the sight of God and before
others—Finney elaborated on the prophet Hosea's word, "Break
up your [fallow] ground; for it is time to seek the LORD" (10:12).

What is it, he asked, to break up the fallow ground? Here is his pointed and searching reply:

> To break up the fallow ground is to *break up your hearts*—to prepare your minds to bring forth fruit unto God. The mind of man is often compared in the Bible to ground, and the word of God to seed sown in it, and the fruit represents the actions and affections of those who receive it. To break up the fallow ground, therefore, is to bring the mind into such a state that it is fitted to receive the word of God. Sometimes your hearts get matted down hard and dry, and all run to waste, till there is no such thing as getting fruit from them till they are all broken up, and mellowed down, and fitted to receive the word of God. It is this softening of the heart, so as to make it feel the truth, which the prophet calls breaking up your fallow ground.

How is the fallow ground to be broken up? *It is not by any direct effort to feel something.* If you mean to break the fallow ground of your heart, you must begin by looking at your heart—examine and note the state of your mind, as to where you stand with God. People talk about religious feeling as if it were something they could by direct effort on their part simply call forth. But this is not the way the mind works. No man can make himself feel a certain way about something merely by *trying* to feel it. Our feelings are not directly under our control, in that we cannot by direct volition call forth religious feelings, but they can be controlled *indirectly*—otherwise there would be no moral character to them.

For example, if a man is away from his family and brings them to mind, will he not feel something? But it is not by saying to himself, *Now I will feel deeply for my family*. A man can direct his attention to any object about which he ought to feel and wishes to feel, and in that way he will call into existence the proper emotions. Let a man call his enemy to mind, and his feelings of enmity toward that one will rise. So if a man thinks of God and fastens his mind on any part of God's character, he will feel something—emotions will come up by the very laws of his mind. If he is a friend of God, let him contemplate God as a gracious and holy being and he will have feelings of friendship. If he is an enemy of God, only let him get the true character of God before his mind and look at it, and fasten his attention on it, and his enmity will rise against God, or he will break down and give his heart to God.

Self-examination consists in looking at your life, considering your actions, calling up the past and learning its true character. Look over your past history. Take up your individual sins one by one and look at them. It is not enough to cast a glance at your past life and see that it has been full of sins and then go to God and make a sort of general confession and ask for pardon. No, take a pen and paper, and write your sins down as they occur to you. Go over them as carefully as a merchant goes over his books; and as often as a sin comes before your mind, add it to the list. General confessions of sin will never do. Your sins were committed one by one, and as far as you can remember, they ought to be reviewed and repented of one by one. Finney listed sins of omission and sins of commission.

Sins of omission

1. *Ingratitude*. Write down under this heading all the instances you can remember where you have received favors from God and never offered thanks: some remarkable providence or wonderful turn of events that saved you from ruin. Put down the instances of God's goodness to you when you were in sin, before your conversion. Then list the mercy of God in the circumstances of your conversion. How many mercies have you received since? How long is the list of instances where God has intervened and you have taken His help for granted? Go to your knees and confess them one by one to God and ask His forgiveness.

2. *Lack of love toward God*. Write down your feelings of love to God for His faithfulness, for his mercy, for forgiveness, for daily provisions, and for salvation—for which you have not always responded in love to Him.

3. *Neglect of the Bible*. The Word of God is our guide for all of

life. If we neglect it, it is no wonder we lose our way or lack courage for the day. You may have put it aside altogether for a period of time, or, if you have read it, you may have done it without knowing what you have read, because you are so preoccupied with other things. Many people read over a whole chapter in such a way that if they were asked when they finished, they could not tell you what they had read.

4. *Unbelief.* Your unbelief of God's express promises and declarations is the same as if you had virtually charged the God of truth with lying.

5. *Neglect of prayer.* Are there times when you have omitted secret prayer, family prayer, and prayer meetings, or have prayed in such a way as to more grievously offend God than if you had neglected it altogether?

6. *Neglect of the means of grace.* When you use trifling excuses for not attending meetings or neglect to avail yourself of every means of receiving God's grace and mercy, you fail to appropriate what God has provided for you.

7. *Performing Christian disciplines in a careless, perfunctory manner.* The manner in which you have done what you know to do for Christian growth will be without effect if it is done without thought or feeling.

8. *Lack of love for the souls of your fellowmen.* If you take an inventory of your friends and family, you may see how little compassion you have felt for their souls. When did you last pray fervently for them or spend a few moments in conversation with them about their spiritual well-being?

9. *Lack of concern for the lost.* Is there genuine concern or prayer or giving of your means for the lost in other countries, or even for those in your own neighborhood or community?

10. *Neglect of family responsibility.* How have you lived before family members? How have you prayed for them and what example or role model have you set before them? Do you make any direct efforts for their spiritual good? Is there any duty toward them you have *not* neglected?

11. *Neglect of social responsibility*. There are times in any community where opportunities are given for social action or interaction. The Christian should take advantage of these times.

12. *Neglect of watchfulness over your own life and character*. Have you ever entirely neglected to watch your conduct, been taken off guard, and sinned before the world, the church, and God?

13. *Neglect to watch over your Christian brothers and sisters*. How often have you broken your covenant to watch over your Christian family in the Lord? How little do you know or care about the state of their souls or temporal needs they may have? How many times have you seen a brother grow cold in his faith and not spoken to him about it or sought to be of assistance in prayer or in some practical way?

14. *Neglect of self-denial*. There are many professors of faith who are willing to do almost anything that does not require self-denial. But when they are called to do something that asks them to deny themselves, it becomes too much. They will not willingly suffer reproach for the name of Christ. Nor will they deny themselves the luxuries of this life to save a world from hell. Some are giving of their abundance and complain that others don't give more, when in truth they do not give enough to suffer any lack.

Sins of commission

1. *Worldly-mindedness*. What is the state of your heart with regard to your earthly possessions? Have you looked at them as *yours*—as if you had a right to dispose of them at will? Have you loved property and sought after it for its own sake or to gratify lust or ambition? If it were all taken away, would you grieve its loss?

2. *Pride*. Recall all the instances you can in which you found yourself full of pride. Vanity is a form of pride. Have you been vain about your dress and appearance? How often have you given more time and effort to adorning your body to go to church than you have to preparing your heart for the worship of God? Have

you gone to the house of God caring more about how you appear outwardly before mortal men than how your soul appears before an all-knowing God?

3. *Envy*. Look at the cases in which you were envious of those whom you thought were above you in any respect. Or perhaps you have envied those who have been more talented or more useful than yourself. Have you ever envied someone so much that it was painful to hear him praised? Has it been more agreeable to you to dwell upon one's faults than upon his virtues, upon his failures than upon his successes? Be honest with yourself, and if you have harbored this spirit, repent deeply before God.

4. *Censoriousness*. This is having a bitter spirit and speaking of Christians in a manner entirely devoid of charity and love—virtues that require you to put the best construction on any dubious conduct.

5. *Slander*. Have you spoken behind people's backs of their faults, real or supposed—of members of the church or others unnecessarily or without good reason? This is slander. You need not lie to be guilty of slander—to tell the truth with intent to injure is also slander.

6. *Levity*. How often have you been flippant before God as you would not have dared to be in the presence of an earthly authority? If you have done this, you have been like an atheist—denying or forgetting that there is a God—or at least you have had less respect for Him and His presence than you would have had for an earthly judge.

7. *Lying*. This is any type of *designed* deception for a selfish reason. If the deception is not by design, it is not lying. But if you mean to make an impression contrary to the naked truth, you lie. Write down all the times you have done this that you can recall. Don't call lies by another name. God calls them *lies* and charges you with lying, and you had better charge yourself correctly.

8. *Cheating*. Think of all the instances in which you have dealt with an individual or done to him that which you would not like to have done to you. *That* is cheating. Another form of cheating is

setting forth something for which you take personal credit that is not yours to take.

9. *Hypocrisy.* This sin can show itself in your prayers and confessions to God. Have you ever prayed for things you did not really want? The evidence of this is that when you have finished praying you could not tell what you had prayed for. How many times have you confessed sins that you did not have any intention of ceasing to commit? Have you ever tried to appear to be someone you are not?

10. *Robbing God.* Are there times when you have misspent time or money—squandered the precious hours God gave you to serve Him or spent money foolishly for that which neither contributed to your health, usefulness, or service? Part of Christian commitment is being a wise steward of time, talents, and resources.

11. *Bad mood or temper.* For lack of proper rest or discipline, you may have spoken harshly to your wife or children, other family members, co-workers, or neighbors. Or you may have developed a habit of displaying a general bad mood or temper. Think of yourself as the only example of a Christlike attitude and life to some of those around you and repent of wrongdoing in this area.

12. *Hindering others from being useful.* Perhaps you have weakened the influence of others by insinuations against them. You have not only robbed God of your own talents but also thwarted the effectiveness of someone else.

If you have committed a fault against an individual, and that individual is within your reach, go and confess the fault to him immediately. If the individual you have injured is too far away for you to go and see him, write him a letter or call him and confess the offense. If you have defrauded anyone, send the money to him in the full amount, with interest.

Do not put off taking care of this; it will only make matters worse. Confess to God those sins that have been committed against God, and to man those sins that have been committed against man. Do not think of getting off lightly by going around the stumbling blocks. Take them out of the way. In breaking up the fallow ground, you must remove every obstruction. Things may be left undone that you consider small and insignificant, and you may wonder why you do not feel more fervent in your faith, when the simple reason is that your proud and carnal mind has covered up that which God has required you to confess and remove. Break up *all* the ground and turn it over.

As you go over the catalog of your sins, resolve to reform in these areas immediately. Wherever you find anything wrong, decide at once that in God's strength you will sin no more in that way. It will be of no benefit to examine yourself unless you determine to amend in every instance what you find wrong in your heart, temper, or conduct.

This breaking up of the fallow ground, this humbling of heart by contrition, repentance, and confession is the first step toward revival. Without this softening of our hard hearts, the Word of God will not take root and there will be no fruit of the Spirit in our lives. Turning over the fallow ground is our responsibility: *"If my people . . . will humble themselves,"* declares the Lord.

If We Pray . . .

The second condition for revival given in 2 Chronicles 7:14 is to *"pray."* After our hearts have been humbled in utter contrition, then prevailing prayer becomes our portion. Early in his Christian life, Finney learned to pray, and out of a lifetime of intercession and service he was qualified to speak on the subject.

Prayer, he said, is an essential link in the chain of causes that leads to a revival, as necessary as truth. Some have zealously used truth to convert men and laid very little stress on prayer. They have preached and talked and distributed tracts with great zeal and then wondered that they had so little success. The reason was that they forgot to use the other branch of the means—effectual prayer. They overlooked the fact that truth by itself will never produce the effect without the Spirit of God, and that the Spirit is given in answer to earnest prayer. Sometimes it happens that those who are the most engaged in employing truth are not the most engaged in prayer. This is unfortunate, for unless they or someone else in cooperation with them have the spirit of prayer, the truth by itself will do nothing but harden the hearts of the hearers in impenitence. It will no doubt be revealed in the day of judgment that nothing was ever done by truth alone, used ever so zealously, unless there was a spirit of prayer somewhere in connection with the presentation of it.

Others err on the other side—not that they lay too much stress on prayer, but they overlook the fact that prayer might be offered forever, and without the presentation of truth, nothing would be done for the unbeliever. Finney listed ways to be effectual in prayer:

1. *One must pray for a definite object.* He need not expect an answer to prayer if he prays at random without any distinct or definite object in mind. Many people go away to their place of prayer because they must *say* their prayers. They are in the habit of going to prayer in the morning or at noon or at whatever time of day it may be, and not having something particular to pray for, they fall down on their knees and pray for whatever comes to mind—whatever floats through their imagination at the time— and when they are done, they can hardly remember a word of what they prayed. This is not effectual prayer.

One must have some plan to his prayers. He cannot pray effectually for a variety of things at once. The mind is so constituted that it cannot dwell intensely upon several things at the same time. All the instances of effectual prayer recorded in the Bible were of the kind that had an object or particular subject in mind. Wherever you see that the blessing sought for in prayer was attained, you will find that the prayer offered was prayer for that particular thing.

2. *Prayer, to be effectual, must be in accordance with the revealed*

will of God. To pray for things contrary to the revealed will of God is to tempt God. There are three ways in which God's will is revealed to men for their guidance in prayer.

(a) Through promises or predictions in the Bible that He will give or do certain things. Some of these are express promises with regard to particular things, and some are promises in general terms that we may apply to particular things.

(b) By His providence. When He makes it clear to us that a given event is about to take place, it is as much a revelation as it would be if it were written in His Word.

(c) By His Spirit. When God's people are unable to see what should be prayed for, His Spirit—in agreement with His will—often instructs them. Where there is no particular revelation, and providence leaves it as such, we are expressly told that "the Spirit helps us in our weakness," and "the Spirit himself intercedes for us with groans that words cannot express" (Romans 8:26).

3. *The one who prays must be in submission to the will of God.* Do not confound submission with indifference and do not confound it with a general confidence that God will do what is right. It is proper to have confidence that God will do what is right in all things, but this is different from submission. What I mean by submission in prayer is acquiescence in the revealed will of God. To submit to any command of God is to obey it.

4. *Effectual prayer for an object implies a desire for that object commensurate with its importance.* If a person *truly* desires any blessing, his desire will bear some proportion to the greatness of the blessing.

(a) If it is a desirable object and if, so far as we can see, it would be an act of benevolence for God to grant it, His general benevolence is presumptive evidence that He will grant it.

(b) If you find yourself filled with benevolent desire for something, there is a strong possibility that the Spirit of God is giving you that desire and is stirring you up to pray for that particular thing so that it may be granted in answer to prayer. In such a case, no degree of desire or importunity in prayer is improper. A Christian may come in prayer and, as it were, take hold of the hand of God. Remember the case of Jacob, when he exclaimed in agony of desire, "I will not let you go unless you bless me"? (Genesis 32:26). Was God displeased with his boldness and importunity? Not at all; He granted him the very thing he prayed for.

Such prayer is offered today when Christians have been stirred to such a state of holy boldness that afterward when they look back upon it they are frightened and amazed to think they dared to exercise such importunity with God. And yet these prayers have prevailed and obtained the blessing. And many of these persons are among the most holy in their Christian walk.

5. *Prayer, to be effectual, must be offered from right motives.* Prayer should not be selfish but dictated by a supreme regard for the glory of God. A great deal of prayer is offered from pure selfishness. Women sometimes pray for their husband that he may be converted, because, as they say, "It would be so much more pleasant to have my husband go to meetings with me." They do not seem to think how their husband is dishonoring God by his sins and how God would be glorified in his conversion. So it is with parents. They cannot bear to think that *their children* should be lost. They pray for them very earnestly indeed. But if you talk with them, they are very tender and tell you how good their children are, how they respect Christianity, and how they think they are *almost* Christians; it is almost as if they are afraid you will hurt their children if you tell them the truth. They do not think how such amiable and lovely children are dishonoring God by their sins; they are only thinking what a dreadful thing it will be for them if they go to hell. Unless their thoughts rise higher than this, their prayers will never prevail with a holy God. The temptation to selfish motives is so strong that there is reason to fear a great many parental prayers never rise above the yearnings of parental sympathy. And that is the reason why so many prayers are not heard and why so many pious praying parents have ungodly children.

6. *Prayer, to be effectual, must be by the intercession of the Spirit.*

You never can expect to offer prayer according to the will of God without the help of the Holy Spirit.

7. *Prayer must be persevering prayer.* In general, Christians who have backslidden and lost the spirit of prayer will not suddenly get into the habit of persevering prayer. Their minds are not in a right state; they cannot focus their minds and hold on until the blessing comes. If they could, they would persevere till the answer comes. True persevering prayer might be offered all at once or it may consist of praying often for something over a period of time.

8. *Effectual prayer requires that one have an intense desire for that which is requested.* The apostle Paul speaks of it as a travail of the soul (Galatians 4:19; 2 Thessalonians 3:8).

9. *If you mean to pray effectually, you must pray often.* It was said of the apostle James that after he died it was discovered that his knees were calloused like those of a camel from praying so much. And there was the secret of the success of those early ministers.

10. *A prayer to be effectual must be offered in the name of Christ.* You cannot come to God in your own name. You cannot plead your own merits. Only the name of Jesus brings results in prayer.

11. *You cannot prevail in prayer without renouncing all your sins.* You must not only recall them to mind but you must actually renounce them, repent of them, and purpose in your heart not to repeat them.

12. *You must pray in faith.* You must expect to obtain the things you ask for. You need not look for an answer to prayer if you pray without any expectation of receiving it.

"If my people, who are called by my name, will humble themselves and *pray* and seek my face and turn from their wicked ways, then will I hear from heaven and will forgive their sin and will heal their land" (2 Chronicles 7:14) is the promise of the Most High. Are we doing our part in prayer? "The prayer of a righteous man is powerful and effective" (James 5:16).

If We Are Spirit-Filled . . .

"Not by might, nor by power, but by my Spirit," said the Almighty through Zechariah to the bruised and bewildered remnant occupied with rebuilding their city and temple in the face of implacable foes. The truth is pertinent for God's people in every generation, for God's work is not dependent on our might or power in the last analysis but on the operation of His Spirit. "If God be for us, who can be against us?"

On the night of his conversion to Christ, Finney knew the fullness of the Spirit in his life, and throughout his ministry he experienced, as we have noted, the frequent outpouring of the Holy Spirit in revival power. He therefore laid great stress on Christians being filled with the Spirit in order to be effective and obedient servants of God.

"Why should the Christian be Spirit-filled?" he inquired, and then made his own reply to the question:

1. *Because you may have the Spirit*. Not because it is a matter of justice for God to give you His Spirit, but because He has promised to give it to those who ask. "If you then, though you are evil, know how to give good gifts to your children, how much more will your Father in heaven give the Holy Spirit to those who ask him?" (Luke 11:13). If you ask for the Holy Spirit, God has promised to give it.

But again, God has commanded you to have it: "Be filled with the Spirit." When God commands us to do a thing, it is the highest possible evidence that we *can* do it. He will not command us to do something unless we have the power to obey it or have access to that power.

2. *It is our duty . . .*

(a) because we have His promise of it

(b) because God has commanded it

(c) because it is essential to our own growth in grace

(d) because it is as important as sanctification

(e) because it is as necessary as our being useful to God and our doing good in the world

(f) because without it we will dishonor God and disgrace the church.

3. *Why many do not have the Spirit*: There are some, even professors of Christ, who will say, "I do not know anything about this; I have never had any such experience; either it is not true or I am all wrong." Following are a few of the reasons that may prevent you from being filled with Spirit:

(a) It may be that you live a hypocritical life. Your prayers are not earnest and sincere. Not only is your religion a mere outside show without any heart but you are also insincere in your relationships with others. Thus you do many things to grieve the Spirit so that he cannot dwell with you.

(b) Others are so flippant that the Spirit will not dwell with them. The Spirit of God is serious and will not dwell with those who live with an attitude of frivolity or foolishness.

(c) Others are so proud that the Spirit will not abide with them. They are so fond of the high life, possessions, fashion, and status that it is little wonder they are not filled with the Spirit. And yet such persons are at a loss to know why it is that they do not enjoy their faith!

(d) Some are so worldly-minded, love property so much, and are trying so hard to get rich, that they cannot have the Spirit. How can He dwell with them when their thoughts are absorbed with the things of the world and all their powers are taken up in procuring wealth?

There is a multitude of such things by which the Spirit of God is grieved. People call them little sins, but God does not call them little. It is the lack of moral principles and prevailing disputes in the church that grieve away the Holy Spirit. God cannot dwell in or have communion with persons who take advantage of others or cheat their neighbor out of his due simply because they can do it without being disgraced.

(e) Others do not fully confess and forsake their sins and so cannot enjoy the Spirit's presence. They will confess their sins in general terms, perhaps, and are ready always to acknowledge that they are sinners, but they will confess only partially some particular sins. When they confess to others the injuries they have done to them, they do it reservedly, proudly, guardedly, as if they were afraid they might say a little more than is necessary. They do it in a way that shows that instead of coming from a full heart, the confession is wrung from them by the hand of conscience. Unless you humble yourself and confess your sins honestly and fully and repay where you have done injury, you have no right to expect the spirit of prayer.

(f) Others are neglecting some known responsibility, and that is the reason why they do not have the Spirit. One does not pray with his family, for instance, though he knows he ought to do it, and yet he is trying to get the spirit of prayer! There is many a young man who feels in his heart that he ought to prepare for the ministry, and he does not have the spirit of prayer because he follows some worldly pursuit instead. He knows his responsibility and refuses to do it, and now he is praying for direction from the Spirit of God! He will not have it.

I have known women who felt that they ought to talk to their unconverted husbands and pray with them, but they have neglected it and so they are in the dark with regard to other things. They know their duty and refuse to do it, and they have lost the spirit of prayer.

If you have neglected any known responsibility, and thus lost the spirit of prayer, you must yield first to what you know is right. God has a controversy with you, and you have refused obedience to God, and you must retract it. You may have forgotten it, but God has not, and you must set yourself to recall it to mind and repent. God will never yield nor grant you his Spirit until you repent of known failure to obey.

(g) Perhaps you have resisted the Spirit of God. Perhaps you are in the *habit* of resisting the Spirit. In preaching when something has been said that speaks to your heart, you resist conviction. Many are willing to hear plain and searching preaching so long as they can apply it to others; a reclusive spirit makes them take satisfaction in hearing others searched and rebuked, but if the truth touch *them*, they cry out that it is too personal and offensive.

(h) The fact may be that you do not on the whole desire the Spirit. There may be things you are not willing to give up. You find that if you wish to have the Spirit of God dwell with you, you must lead a different life; you must give up the world, you must make sacrifices, you must break off from your worldly associates, and make confession of your sins. And so you do not choose to have Him come, unless He will consent to dwell with you and let you live as you please. But that He will never do.

(i) Perhaps you do not pray for the Spirit at all, or you pray and use no other means, or pray and do not act consistently with your prayers. Or you use means calculated to resist Him. Or you ask, and as soon as He comes and begins to work in your heart, you grieve Him away and will not walk with Him.

4. *The guilt that comes from not having the Spirit of God.*

(a) Your guilt is just as great as the authority of God is great, which commands you to be filled with the Spirit. God commands it, and it is just as much a disobedience of God's commands as it would be to swear profanely or steal or commit adultery or break the Sabbath. Think of that. And yet there are many people who do not blame themselves at all for not having the Spirit. They even think themselves quite pious Christians because they go to prayer meetings and partake of the sacrament, and yet they live year after year without the Spirit of God.

(b) Your guilt is equal to all the good you might do if you had the Spirit of God in as great a measure as it is your duty to have it and as you might have it. Here is a blessing promised, and you can have it by simple obedience. You are entirely responsible to the church and to God for all the good you might do if you had the Spirit.

(c) Your guilt is further measured by all you do halfheartedly in consequence of not having the Spirit. You dishonor your church. You may even be a stumbling block to the church and to the world. And your guilt is enhanced by all the various influences you exert apart from the Spirit of God.

5. *The consequences of having the Spirit*.

(a) You may be called eccentric, and you may deserve it. The reason is that people who are truly filled with the Spirit are unlike other people. They act under different influences, take different views, are moved by different motives, and are led by a different spirit.

(b) If you have much of the Spirit of God, you may even be called crazy by the world. Paul was accused of being so by those who did not understand the basis from which he acted. It is true that Festus thought he was crazy and that much learning had made him mad: "You are out of your mind, Paul! . . . Your great learning is driving you insane." But Paul said, "I am not insane, most excellent Festus. . . ." (Acts 26:24–25). So make up your mind that you may be misunderstood.

(c) If you have the Spirit of God, you must expect to feel distress about the state of the church and the world. Some ask for the Spirit because they think it will make them perfectly happy. Some think spirit-filled Christians are always content and free from sorrow.

This is a great misconception. Read your Bible and see how the prophets and apostles were distressed over the moral condition of the church and the world. The apostle Paul said he always bore in his body the dying of the Lord Jesus. By the Spirit you will know what it is to sympathize with the Lord Jesus Christ and be baptized with the baptism that He was baptized with. Oh, how He agonized over the state of sinners! How He travailed in soul for their salvation! The more you have of His Spirit, the more clearly you will understand this and the more deeply you will grieve over the lost.

(d) You will often grieve over the state of the ministry. Some years ago I met a woman belonging to one of the churches in this city. I inquired of her the state of the church. She seemed unwilling to say much about it, made some general remarks, and then she became choked up and her eyes filled with tears. She said the minister's mind seemed to be very dark. Spiritual Christians often feel like this, and often weep. Then they have the added burden of not saying too much lest they grieve the Spirit by speaking anything against others.

(e) If you have the Spirit of God, you must make up your mind that you will have opposition, both in the church and in the world. Very likely even the leading men in the church will oppose you. There has always been opposition in the church. It was so when Christ was on earth. If you are very far above their level of experience, church members will oppose you. If any man will live godly in Christ Jesus he must expect persecution. Often the elders, and even the pastor himself, will oppose you if you are filled with the Spirit of God and they are not.

(f) You must expect very frequent and agonizing conflicts with Satan. Satan has very little trouble with Christians who are not spiritual—who are lukewarm, even slothful and worldly minded. But spiritual Christians are doing him a great injury, which he knows very well and so he sets himself against them. Such Christians will have temptations they never dreamed of: blasphemous thoughts, atheistic tendencies, suggestions to do wicked deeds—to destroy their own lives or those of others. If you are a spiritual Christian, you may expect these temptations and conflicts.

(g) You will have greater conflicts with yourself than you ever thought possible. You will sometimes find your own carnality making strange headway against the Spirit. "For the sinful nature desires what is contrary to the Spirit, and the Spirit what is contrary to the sinful nature." Such a Christian is often thrown into consternation over the power of his own flesh.

(h) But you will have peace with God. Though many may oppose you, there will be One with whom you will have peace. Let those who are called to these trials, conflicts, and temptations, and who groan within themselves in prayer, their hearts broken before God, remember this: Your peace, so far as your feelings toward God are concerned, will flow like a river.

(i) If you are led by the Spirit, you will likewise have peace of conscience. You will not be constantly plagued with guilt but will experience the calm and quiet of a summer's lake.

(j) And if you are filled with the Spirit, you will be useful to God. You cannot help it. Even if you were sick and unable to leave your home or to converse with anyone, you would be ten times more useful than those who do not know the filling of the Spirit of God.

(k) When people speak against you, if you are filled with the Spirit, you will not find yourself distressed and worried over it. When people are easily irritated and fret over any little thing that touches them, I think they have surely *not* been filled with the Spirit of Christ. Jesus Christ had everything said against Him that malice could invent and yet was not in the least disturbed by it. If you want to be meek under persecution and exemplify the temper of the Savior, you need to be filled with the Spirit.

(l) You will be wise in dealing with sinners and in leading them toward a conversion experience. If the Spirit of God is in you, He will lead you in a way adapted to the needs of the hearer to avoid doing them any harm or offending them in any way.

(m) You will be calm under affliction, not thrown into confusion or consternation when storms arise. People around you will be astonished at your calmness and cheerfulness under heavy trials, not knowing the inward support of those who are filled with the Spirit.

(n) You will be resigned even in death; you will always feel prepared to die and not be afraid, your destiny being assured with the prospect of joy forever.

6. *The consequences of not being filled with the Spirit.*

(a) You will often doubt whether you are a Christian. The sons of God are led by the Spirit of God, so it stands to reason that if you are *not* led by the Spirit, what reason do you have to think you are a son?

(b) You will be unsettled regarding your views about the prayer of faith. The prayer of faith is spiritual, a matter of experience and not speculation. Unless you are spiritual, you will not understand it fully. You may talk a great deal about it, and for a time even be thoroughly convinced of it, but you will not feel settled enough about it so as to retain a constant frame of mind concerning it.

(c) If you do not have the Spirit, you will be very apt to stumble at those who do. You will doubt the propriety of their conduct. You will perhaps doubt their sincerity. You will try to censure them for the purpose of justifying yourself.

(d) You will fall into line with the impenitent and the carnal. They will praise you as a rational, orthodox, consistent Christian, and you will fill inclined to walk with them because you are agreed.

(e) You will be troubled with fears about fanaticism. When there are revivals, you will tend to be full of fear and anxiety about them or you will be in opposition to them.

(f) You will be disturbed by the strategies used in revivals. If new ones are adopted, you may stumble at them in proportion to your lack of spirituality.

(g) You will become a reproach to Christianity. The impenitent will sometimes praise you because you are so much like them and other times laugh at you because you are a hypocrite.

(h) You will truly know very little about the Word of God.

Not to be filled with the Spirit is to be a weak, wavering, fearful, superficial, and ineffective Christian. Not to be filled with the Spirit is to overlook God's provision or be ignorant of it or despise it. Conversely, to be filled with the Spirit is to be a strong, steady, courageous, established, effective believer, dependent on His strength, yielded to His will, and used for the Savior's glory.

6

The Perils of Revival

Seasons of revival can be hindered by opposition—human and satanic—before they begin or after they have gotten under way. It is the view of some that revivals are miracles of divine grace and power that can neither be promoted nor hindered by the attitudes and actions of men or demons, but such a concept does not line up with the experience of the Christian church over the centuries. It may seem strange to us that man could interfere with a work of God so that it would cease or that the Enemy of our souls could distract or divert the obedience and cooperation of people with the Spirit of God so that revival efforts would be defeated. But what did the apostle to the Gentiles mean by declaring, "For we wanted to come to you—certainly I, Paul, did, again and again— but Satan stopped us" (1 Thessalonians 2:18)?

Is It True That Revivals Can Be Hindered?

Edwards and Finney, out of wide and deep experience, wrote extensively on this matter of hindrances to revival. Let us read and ponder their words and by them search out our own hearts.

We will hear Finney's testimony first, and add the pointed paragraphs prepared by the preacher of Northampton, Jonathan Edwards:

It has always been the case that whenever any servant of God does anything in His cause and it appears that his efforts will succeed, Satan through his agents will attempt to divert that one's mind and nullify his labors. So it has been during the last ten years, in which there have been such remarkable revivals through the length and breadth of the land. These revivals have been very powerful and very extensive. It has been estimated that not less than two hundred thousand have been converted to God during this time. And the devil has been busy diverting and distracting the people of God, even depleting their energies from pushing forward the great work of salvation.

There are several things that can put a stop to a revival.

Some have spoken carelessly on this subject, as if nothing could thwart a genuine revival. They say that if a revival is a work of God, it cannot be stopped: Can any created being stop God? But thinking it through, is this really common sense? It was formerly an established belief that a revival could not be stopped because it was the work of God. Everyone supposed that it would go on whatever was done to hinder it, in the church or out of it. But the farmer might just as well reason that he could cut down his wheat and not hurt the crop because it is God that makes grain grow. A revival is the work of God, and so is a crop of wheat; and God is as much dependent on the use of means in one case as the other. And, therefore, a revival is just as liable as a wheat field to be hindered or cut short.

1. *A revival will stop when church members believe it is going to stop.* Church members are the instruments God uses to carry on His work, and they must work at it voluntarily and with their whole hearts. Nothing is more damaging to a revival than for those involved in it to predict that it is going to end. If such an idea takes root and it is not counteracted, the revival will certainly end.

2. *A revival will cease when Christians consent that it should.* Sometimes Christians will see that a revival is waning and that if something isn't done it will come to a standstill. If this fact distresses them and drives them to prayer and to fresh commitment to remain in the Spirit, the work will not cease. When Christians love the work of God and the salvation of souls enough that they are distressed at the mere thought of a move of the Spirit waning, they will do what is necessary to see it continue. If no effort to avert its ending or to renew the work occurs, they are as much as consenting that it should cease.

3. *A revival will end when Christians become mechanical in their attempts to promote it.* When their faith is strong and their hearts and prayers are full of holy enthusiasm and power, the work will go on. But when their prayers begin to grow cold and they must labor in the flesh to produce them, then the revival will cease.

4. *The revival will cease when Christians embrace the idea that the work will go on without their input.* Church members are co-workers with God in promoting a revival, and the work will go on at the pace and to the extent that the church allows and no more. Sinners cannot be converted apart from their own free will, for conversion consists in their voluntarily turning to God. And neither can sinners be converted without hearing the Word preached and receiving some influence of God's people to encourage them in their choice. God does not convert the world by physical omnipotence. He is dependent on the moral influence of the church.

5. *The work will cease when church members prefer to attend to their own concerns rather than to God's business.* I am not saying that men have any business that is exclusively their own, but they think they do and, in fact, generally prefer to serve their own pursuits rather than to work for God. They begin to think they cannot afford the time that is necessary from their worldly employments to carry on a revival. And they contend they are bound to give up attending to the things of God because of earthly obligations. When this happens, of course, the revival comes to a halt.

6. *When Christians become proud of a great revival, it will cease.*

I refer to those Christians who have before been instrumental in promoting it. Perhaps it has been published in the newspapers: "What a revival there has been in [such and such a] church" and "How involved the members have been. . . ." And they think how highly they shall be regarded in the estimation of other churches all over the area because they have had such a great revival. And so they become puffed up and vain and they can no longer enjoy the presence of God. So the Spirit withdraws from them and the revival ceases.

7. *The revival will stop when the church becomes overworked*. Multitudes of Christians commit a great error in times of revival. They are so careless and use so little good judgment that they disrupt their normal habits of living, neglecting to eat and sleep and rest at the proper times. They allow the excitement of the revival to carry them away, and they overwork their bodies and soon become exhausted, making it impossible for them to continue in the work.

8. *A revival will cease when the church begins to speculate about abstract doctrines, which have nothing to do with practice*. If church members turn their attention from the things of salvation and go to studying or disputing abstract points, the revival will not go forward.

9. *When Christians begin to proselytize, it is the beginning of the end of God's working in their midst*. When the Baptists are so opposed to the Presbyterians, or the Presbyterians to the Baptists, or both against the Methodists, or the Episcopalians against the rest, that they begin to make efforts to get the converts to join their church and avoid the others, you will see the last of a revival.

10. *When Christians refuse to render to the Lord according to the benefits they have received, the work of the Spirit will see a cooling down*. This is a source of religious declension. God opens the windows of heaven on a church, pouring out a blessing on all, and He reasonably expects tithes and offerings to come into the storehouse to further the work of Zion. When the church basks in God's glory and blessing but withholds its bounty and earthly re-

sources, they have grieved the Spirit of God and the blessing is withdrawn.

11. *When the church in any way grieves the Holy Spirit, He cannot abide with them.*

(a) When they do not feel dependent on the Spirit but rather become strong in their own strength, God withdraws His blessings. In many instances, Christians sin against themselves when they become lifted up with their own success and take the credit for it, not giving God the glory. There is doubtless a great temptation toward this, and it requires the utmost watchfulness on the part of ministers and churches to guard against it and not to grieve the Spirit away by boasting in their own accomplishments.

(b) Some, under pretense of publishing things to the praise and glory of God, have published articles that strongly exalted themselves and their efforts. In the revival of this city four years ago, so much was said in the papers that appeared to be self-exalting that I was afraid to publish anything. I am not speaking against the practice itself of publishing accounts of revivals. But the *manner* of doing it is of vast importance. If it is done so as to promote pride, it renders a fatal blow to the revival.

(c) To publish things that are calculated to devalue the work of God is to grieve the Spirit of God. When an obvious work of God is spoken lightly of, not rendering to God the glory due His name, the Spirit is grieved. If anything is said about a revival, let only the plain facts be related just as they occurred, and let the reader judge who is the author of them.

12. *A revival may be expected to cease when Christians lose the spirit of brotherly love.* Jesus Christ will not continue with people in a revival any longer than they continue in the exercise of brotherly love. When Christians are in the spirit of revival, they will feel love toward their brothers. I never saw a revival in which this was not the case. But as soon as this begins to cease, the Spirit of God is grieved and departs.

13. *A revival will decline and cease unless Christians are frequently humbled before God.* By this I mean that Christians, in

order to keep in the spirit of a revival, commonly need to be convicted, humbled, and broken down before God. This is something that many do not understand. They suppose that once a person is converted there is no need for further conviction and repentance, but the fact is that in a revival the Christian's heart is capable of becoming resistant and losing its exquisite relish for divine things; his unction and prevalence in prayer abates, and he must be bathed in a fresh work of the Holy Spirit. It is impossible to keep one in such a state of humilty so as not to do injury to the work, unless he goes through such a process frequently throughout the revival. Revivals decline because those in the church do not see their need to remain in dependence upon the Holy Spirit, in humility before God, seeking to know how they might further submit to His leading.

14. *A revival cannot continue when Christians do not practice self-denial.* When the church has enjoyed a revival and members begin to grow satisfied, they often run into self-indulgence and take for granted the sacrifice of the Son of God, who gave up all to save sinners. Unless they are willing to give up their luxuries and their ease and lay their lives down for the work, they cannot expect the Spirit of God to continually pour himself out upon them.

15. *A revival will be stopped by controversies about new measures.* Nothing is more certain to overthrow a revival than this. All must remain in submission to the Holy Spirit and to the ways and means He chooses to revive His people.

16. *Revivals can be put down by the continued opposition of the "old school," combined with a bad spirit in the "new school."* If those who do nothing to promote revivals continue their opposition, and if those who are laboring to promote them allow themselves to become impatient and adopt a bad spirit, the revival will surely cease. Let those who promote revivals keep about their work and not talk about the opposition—or preach or print about it. If others choose to publish their complaints for all to see, let the Lord's servants keep to their work just the same. All the writ-

ing and slander will not stop a revival borne of the Holy Spirit while those who are engaged in it mind their business and keep to their work.

But whenever those who are actively engaged in promoting a revival become agitated at the unreasonableness and tenacity of the opposition and lose their patience, and feel as if they must answer their slanderers, then they have lowered themselves to the level of their accusers, and the work must cease.

17. *Any diversion of the public mind will hinder a revival.* Anything that succeeds in significantly diverting public attention will put a stop to a revival. Even if an angel from heaven were to come down and appear in the streets, it might be the worst thing in the world for a revival, for it would turn sinners from their conviction and the church from praying for souls to follow this glorious being . . . and that would be the end of the revival.

18. *Neglect of the claims of missions is another hindrance to revival.* If Christians do not feel a burden for the heathen or use the means available to them to become informed on the subject, and if they reject the light that God is showing them, not being willing to do what God calls them to do in this regard, the Spirit of God will depart from them.

19. *When a church rejects the call of God upon it for the education of young people for the ministry, it will hinder and destroy a revival.* Churches do not generally press upon young people the duty of going into the ministry. God pours His Spirit on the churches and converts hundreds of souls, and if from this result the laborers do not come forth into the harvest, what can be expected but that the curse of God will come upon the churches and His Spirit will be withdrawn and revivals will cease?

20. *Slandering revivals will often put them down.* The great revival in the days of Jonathan Edwards suffered greatly from the conduct of the church in this respect. It is to be expected that the enemies of God will revile, misrepresent, and slander revivals. But when the *church* engages in this work, and many of her most influential members are aiding and abetting in gossip and

misrepresentation of the glorious work of God, it is reasonable that the Spirit will be grieved away.

21. *Ecclesiastical difficulties are calculated to grieve the Holy Spirit and to destroy revivals*. It has always been the policy of the devil to turn the attention of ministers from the work of the Lord to disputes and ecclesiastical litigations. Some of the most efficient ministers in the church have been called off from their direct efforts to win souls to Christ to attend day after day, and in some instances week after week, to charges against them or fellow laborers in the ministry that should never have been sustained.

22. *Another thing by which revivals may be hindered is censoriousness on either side, and especially in those who have been engaged in carrying forward a revival*. It is to be expected that those who oppose a work will watch for error on the part of its promoters and be sure to censure them for all that is wrong—and not infrequently for that which is right in their conduct. It will be particularly expected that many censorious and unchristian remarks will be made about those who are the most prominent instruments in promoting the work. This censoriousness on the part of those who oppose the work, whether in or out of the church, will not in itself put a stop to the revival. Rather, it is when there is retaliation and evil for evil done on the part of God's people that real harm results. While a revival's promoters keep humble and in a prayerful spirit, and while they do not retaliate but possess their souls in patience, not allowing themselves to be diverted, to recriminate, or to grieve away the spirit of prayer, the work will go forward.

Jonathan Edwards learned that *censoriousness*, especially toward other professing Christians, was "the worst disease that has attended this work, most contrary to the spirit and rules of Christianity, and of the worst consequences." Not only were church members tempted to be exceedingly critical of other Christians who in their opinion created the appearance of being converted, but ministers of the gospel treated fellow ministers as those who should be cast out of the church, just as Christ scourged the buyers and sellers in the temple. This attitude he (Jonathan Edwards) held to be erroneous and unchristian. What man knows who in reality is saved or who will be saved, even though at the moment one may be a persecutor of the church, as was Saul of Tarsus? One can sense the deep heart-wounds suffered by the sensitive and sweet-spirited Edwards in his observations on the caustic and destructive spirit of censure:

> God seems strictly to have forbidden the practice of judging our brethren in the visible church, not only because He knows that we are babes, infinitely too weak, fallible, and blind to be well capacitated for it, but also because He knows that it is not a work suited to our proud hearts, that it would be setting us far too high and making us lords over our fellow-creatures. Judging our brethren and passing a condemnatory sentence upon them, seems to carry in it an act of authority, especially in so great a case, to sentence them with respect to that state of their hearts on which depends their liableness to eternal damnation, as is evident by such interrogations as those (to hear which from God's mouth is enough to make us shrink into nothing with shame and confusion, and a sense of our own blindness and worthlessness). Romans 14:4: "Who art thou that judgest another man's servant? to his own master he standeth or falleth." And James 4:12: "There is one lawgiver, who is able to save and to destroy: who art thou that judgest another?" Our wise and merciful Shepherd has graciously taken care not to lay in our way such a temptation to pride; he has cut up all such poison out of our pasture; and therefore we should not desire to have it restored. . . .
>
> This bitter root of censoriousness must be totally pulled out, as we would prepare the way of the Lord. It has nourished and upheld many other things contrary to the humility, meekness, and love of the gospel. The minds of many have received an unhappy turn, in some respects, with their religion. There is a certain point or sharpness, a disposition to a kind of warmth that does not savor of that meek, lamblike, sweet dis-

position that becomes Christians. Many have now been so long habituated to it, that they do not know how to get out of it; but we must get out of it; the point and sharpness must be blunted, and we must learn another way of manifesting our zeal for God.

Edwards, like Finney, learned by experience that spiritual pride underlies many of the difficulties that impede the progress of revivals. Every heart that is hungry for revival should heed his earnest and eloquent warning:

> Spiritual pride disposes [itself] to speak of other persons' sins, their enmity against God and His people, the miserable delusion of hypocrites and their enmity against vital piety, and the deadness of some saints, with bitterness or with laughter and levity and an air of contempt, whereas pure Christian humility disposes one either to be silent about them or to speak of them with grief and pity. . . .
>
> In a situation such as this, it has been the manner in some places, or at least the manner of some persons, to speak of almost everything that they see amiss in others in the most harsh, severe, and offensive language. It is common for them to say of others' opinions or conduct or advice, or of their coldness, their silence, their caution, their moderation, and their prudence—and many other things that appear in them— that they are from the devil or from hell, that such a thing is devilish or hellish or cursed, and that such persons are serving the devil or the devil is in them, and they are soul-murderers and the like; so the words *devil* and *hell* are almost continually in their mouths. And such language they will commonly use, not only toward wicked men but also toward them that they themselves allow to be the true children of God, and also toward ministers of the gospel and others that are very much their superiors. And they look upon it a virtue and high attainment thus to behave themselves. "Oh [they say], we must be plain-hearted and bold for Christ, we must declare war against sin wherever we see it; we must not mince the matter in the cause of God and when speaking for Christ." And to make any

distinction in persons, or to speak the more tenderly, because that which is amiss is seen in a superior, they look upon as very mean for a follower of Christ when speaking in the cause of his Master.

What a strange device of the devil it is to overthrow all Christian meekness and gentleness, and even all show and appearance of it, and to defile the mouths of the children of God, and to introduce the language of common sailors among the followers of Christ under a cloak of high sanctity and zeal and boldness for Christ! And it is a remarkable instance of the weakness of the human mind, and how much too cunning the devil is for us!

The eminently humble Christian is, as it were, clothed with lowliness, mildness, meekness, gentleness of spirit and behavior, and with a soft, sweet, condescending, winning air and deportment; these things are just like garments to him, he is clothed all over with them. "And be clothed with humility. Put on, therefore, as the elect of God, holy and beloved, bowels of mercies, kindness, humbleness of mind, meekness, long suffering."

Pure Christian humility has no roughness or contempt or fierceness or bitterness in its nature; it makes a person like a little child—harmless and innocent—that none need be afraid of; or like a lamb, destitute of all wrath, anger, and clamor, agreeable to Ephesians 4:31.

Unbelief, ease, unconcern, selfishness, ingratitude, pride, controversy, slander, censoriousness, such are the stumbling blocks to revival, the millstones about the neck of the unsaved. "If the Christians are so contentious among themselves and so unconcerned about us, why should we become Christians?" reason the unregenerate, and not without cause. A primary responsibility of believers is to put first the kingdom of God and the salvation of the lost and last themselves with their inconsequential differences and disagreements. Like our Savior, we cannot save others and ourselves too.

What About "New Measures"?

While there are generally recognized spiritual principles of operation in the coming and spread of a revival movement of God's Spirit, there need not be a maintenance of old practices and procedures. It appears from a study of revival in different centuries that the principles are the same, but the methods may vary quite widely from age to age and place to place. It is as though the Most High would break the mold of our ecclesiastical procedure so that there can be the flow of His Spirit into thirsty hearts. "New measures" seems to come up in every great revival effort to be strenuously opposed by some who have confused spiritual life with certain church ritual or order and to be favored enthusiastically by those who see new channels for the divine Spirit. For example, in Edwards' day there was caustic criticism because the converts testified publicly and gladly, a custom little known at that time, or because hymns were substituted for the metrical version of the Psalms, which had been sung for centuries.

Still others found fault with the novelty of special meetings for children, a practice up to that time quite unknown. To this day there are still those who believe that evangelism has no message for little children, despite the demonstrated effectiveness of Child Evangelism, Youth Gospel Crusades, and similar efforts to bring the Savior to the little ones. More than two centuries ago the learned and patient Edwards answered such criticism:

> I have seen many happy effects of children's religious meetings; and God has seemed often remarkable to own them in their meetings, and really descended from heaven to be among them. I have known several probable instances of children being converted at such meetings. I should therefore think that if children appear to be really moved to it by a religious disposition, and not merely from a childish affectation of imitating grown persons, they ought by no means to be discouraged or embarrassed: but yet it is fitting that care should be taken of them by their parents and pastors to instruct and direct them, and to correct impolite or rough conduct if it is per-

ceived, or anything by which the devil may pervert or destroy the design of their meetings. All should take heed that they do not find fault with or despise the simple faith of children, lest they should be like the chief priests and scribes who were displeased at the worship and praises of little children and the honor they gave Christ in the temple.

Finney faced many critics because of innovations he brought into the course of revival services, such as "anxious meetings," "protracted meetings," and the "anxious seat," much as Moody was derided for the "altar call" and Billy Sunday for his "sawdust trail." Finney made pertinent reply in his *Lectures on Revivals of Religion* to the effect:

1. *If we examine the history of the church, we will find that there never has been an extensive reformation except by new measures.* Whenever the churches get settled down into a *form* of doing things, they soon come to rely upon the outward doing of it and so retain the form of religion while they lose the substance. And so it has always been impossible to awaken them to bring about a reformation of the faults in the church and to produce a revival, simply by pursuing established forms. Perhaps it is not too much to say that it is impossible for God himself to bring about reformations except by new measures.

2. *The same distinctions, in substance, that now exist have always existed in all seasons of reformation and revival.* There have always been those who particularly adhered to their forms and notions and precise way of doing things, as if they had a "Thus saith the Lord" for every one of them.

In such cases, the churches have gradually lost their confidence in opposition to new measures, and the cry of "innovation" has ceased to alarm them. They see that the blessing of God is with those who are accused of new measures and innovation, and the continued opposition of the "old school," together with the continued success of the "new school," has destroyed their confidence in opposition.

3. *The present cry against new measures is highly ridiculous*

when we consider the quarter from which it comes and all the circumstances in the case. It is truly astonishing that ministers should feel alarmed at the new measures of the present day, as if new measures were something new under the sun, and as if the present form and manner of doing things had descended from the apostles, and were established by a "Thus saith the Lord," when the truth is that every step of the church's advance from the gross darkness of popery has been through the introduction of one new measure after another.

4. *We can see why it is that those who have been making the ado about new measures have not been successful in promoting revivals.* They have been taken up with the distressing factors, real or imaginary, that have attended this great and blessed work of God. That there have been such factors, no one will pretend to deny. While men are taken up with the faults instead of the excellencies of a blessed work of God, how can it be expected that they will be useful in promoting it? I would say all this in great kindness, but still it is a point upon which I must not be silent.

5. *Without new measures, it is impossible that the church will succeed in gaining the attention of the world to the Christian faith.* The measures of politicians, of infidels and heretics, the scrambling after wealth, the increase of luxury, and the ten thousand exciting and counteracting influences that bear upon the church and upon the world will gain their attention and turn all men away from the sanctuary and from the altars of the Lord, unless we increase in wisdom and piety and wisely adopt such new measures as are calculated to get the attention of men to the gospel of Christ. I have already said in the course of these lectures that new measures should be introduced no faster than they are really called for. They should be introduced with the greatest wisdom and caution and prayerfulness, and in a manner calculated to provoke as little opposition as possible. But new measures we *must have.* And may God prevent the church from settling down in *any* set of forms and making the present or any other edition of her measures stereotyped.

6. *It is evident that we must have more stimulating preaching to meet the character and wants of our times.* Ministers are generally beginning to find this out. And some of them complain about it, and suppose it to be owing to "new measures," as they call them. The character of our times has changed, and these men have not conformed to it, but retain the same stiff, dry, posing style of preaching that answered people's needs half a century ago.

7. *We see the importance of having young ministers obtain the right view of revivals.* In many cases I have seen that great pains are taken to discourage young men who are preparing for the ministry, warning them about the faults of revivals, the new measures, and the like. In fact, in some theological seminaries they are taught to look upon new measures as if they were inventions of the devil. How can these men know true revival when they are taught such things? Some are frightened to death about new measures, as if there had never been any such thing as a new way of doing something. They ought to know that new methods are not a new thing in the church.

We need to teach a young minister to enter fully into his work, to pour out his heart to God for His blessing. Whenever he sees the lack of any measure to bring the truth more powerfully before the minds of the people, let him adopt it and not be afraid. If ministers will not go forward and preach the gospel with power and earnestness, and will not go out of their way to do anything *new* for the purpose of saving souls, they will surely grieve the Holy Spirit, and God will raise up other ministers to do His work in the world.

8. *It is the right and duty of ministers to adopt new measures for promoting revivals.* In some places church members have opposed their minister when he has attempted to employ those measures that God has blessed for a revival, and have gone so far as to give up their prayer meetings and their labors to save souls, and to stand aloof from everything because their minister has adopted what they call "new measures." And thus they fall by the wayside and grieve away the Spirit of God, and may even put a stop to the

revival, while the world around them is going to hell.

Finally, this zealous adherence to particular forms and modes of doing things, which has led the church to resist innovative measures, savors strongly of fanaticism. And what is not a little odd is that fanatics of this stamp are always the first to cry out "fanaticism."

The only thing insisted upon under the gospel dispensation in regard to measures is that there should be decency and order. "Let all things be done decently and in order." We are required to guard against all confusion and disorderly conduct. But what is decency and order? Will it be pretended that an anxious meeting or a protracted meeting or an anxious seat is inconsistent with decency and order? I would most sincerely disapprove and firmly resist whatever was indecent and disorderly in the worship of God. But I do not suppose that by "order" we are to understand any particular set mode in which any church may have been accustomed to perform its service.

Granted "decency and order" in revival services, can we not allow the details of method to be left to the guidance of God's Spirit in His chosen instruments?

Must There Be "Excesses"?

One of the greatest complaints of the unconverted against revival in the church is the apparent abuse of emotion, which allegedly brings in its train all manner of "excesses." The practice of Christianity, say the unsaved, should be dignified, reserved, intellectual, aesthetic, and ritualistic. It should portray the beautiful in life and present the noble; it should interpret the works of the Creator and consider the thoughts of cultured men; it should appeal to the intellect and not to the emotions. Away with excitement, they say, it has no place in the worship of God!

Finney learned that apart from enthusiasm men are not stirred to take a stand on a given issue, be it political or religious.

Our physical and mental makeup is such that we are inclined to be spiritually sluggish until our feelings are deeply stirred. God has found it necessary to take advantage of mankind's emotions to produce sufficient enthusiasm among them to obey. Men by nature are spiritually sluggish, and there are so many things to lead their minds away from spiritual things and to oppose the influence of the gospel. They must be so enthused that they will break through these counteracting influences in order to obey God. Not that emotional feelings *constitute* religion, for they certainly do not. But the will is enslaved by carnal and worldly desires until it is awakened to a sense of guilt and danger.

Many good men have supposed, and still suppose, that the best way to promote the faith is to go along *uniformly* and gather in the ungodly gradually and without any emotional fanfare. But however sound such reasoning may appear in the abstract, *facts* demonstrate its futility. If the church were far enough advanced in knowledge and had stability of principle enough to *keep awake*, such a course would do, but this is not the case, and so we endeavor to awaken the church to action through the power of preaching and appeal to the emotions as well as the intellect.

Along with Finney, we grant that revival is liable to the dangers of abuses. He said, "In cases of great *religious* as well as other excitements, more or less incidental evils may be expected, of course. But this is not reason enough that [the revivals] should be given up. The best things are always liable to abuses."

A study of revivals in various centuries and in many countries shows that the emotional reaction of believers and unbelievers to the presence and power of God's Spirit varies to a considerable extent with the traits of individuals and communities. In the Second American Awakening, early in the nineteenth century, the revivals at Yale under President Timothy Dwight were almost entirely without outward manifestation. The Spirit of God came as the dew from heaven—quiet, gentle, not observed by eye or felt by hand; but hearts were melted before God and tears of penitence flowed silently. During the same years the frontier revivals in Kentucky and Tennessee were accompanied by extreme emotional "excesses"—faintings, outcries, barking, "jerks." When the Spirit of God came to us at Wheaton College in 1950, there was heavenly stillness, no shouting or loud crying, no frenzy, no "tongues," only the soft sobbing of broken hearts and the silent flow of tears.

Revival should be the deepest desire of the Christian and in no way a source of apprehension. Should we be afraid of God? The preaching that is aimed only at the emotions is bound to be superficial and fleeting in its effectiveness, while the preaching of the Word in the power of God's Spirit will stir the feelings to the end that hearts will turn to the Savior.

A classic reply to those unduly concerned about possible excesses and errors in times of awakening was made by the saintly Robert Murray McCheyne in his letter to the Presbytery of Aberdeen in Scotland, December 1840. (McCheyne was a contemporary of Finney, although not an acquaintance. Revivals in Britain and on the Continent often have coincided with awakenings in America.) Because of the importance and pertinence of the material in question, it is presented in full, except for minor editing, for the sake of clarity. Also, answers are given after each question, and not separately as in the original.

1. *Have revivals taken place in your parish or district; and if so, to what extent and by what instrumentality and means?*

Answer: It is my decided and solemn conviction, in the sight of God, that a very remarkable and glorious work of God in the conversion of sinners and the edifying of saints has taken place in this parish and neighborhood. This work I have observed going on from the very beginning of my ministry in this place in November 1836, and it has continued to the present time; but it was much more remarkable in the autumn of 1839, when I was abroad on a Mission of Inquiry to the Jews, and when my place was occupied by the Rev. W. C. Burns. Previous to my going abroad, and for several months afterward, the means used were of the ordinary kind. In addition to the services of the Sabbath, in the summer of

1837, a meeting was opened in the church on Thursday evenings for prayer, exposition of the Scripture, reading accounts of missions, revivals of religion, and so forth; Sabbath schools were formed, private prayer meetings were encouraged, and two weekly classes for young men and young women were instituted with a very large attendance. These means were accompanied with an evident blessing from on high in many instances.

But there was no visible or general movement among the people until August 1839, when immediately after the beginning of the Lord's work at Kilsyth, the Word of God came with such power to the hearts and consciences of the people here, and their thirst for hearing it became so intense, that the evening classes in the schoolroom were changed into densely crowded congregations in the church, and for nearly four months it was found desirable to have public worship almost every night. At this time also many prayer meetings were formed, some of which were strictly private or fellowship meetings, and others, conducted by persons of some Christian experience, were open to people concerned about their souls. At the time of my return from the Mission to the Jews, I found thirty-nine such meetings held weekly in connection with the congregation, and five of these were conducted and attended entirely by small children. At present, although many changes have taken place, I believe the number of these meetings is not much diminished. Now, however, they are nearly all of the more private kind—the deep and general conviction, which led to many of them being open, having in a great degree subsided.

As to the extent of this work of God, I believe it is impossible to speak decidedly. The parish is situated in the suburb of a city of 60,000. The work extended to individuals residing in all quarters of the town, and belonging to all ranks and denominations of the people. Many hundreds, under deep concern for their souls, have come, from first to last, to converse with the ministers, so that I am deeply persuaded the number of those who have received saving benefit is greater than anyone will know till Judgment Day.

2. *Do you know the previous character and habits of the parties converted?*

3. *Have any who were notorious for drunkenness or other immoralities, neglect of family duties or public ordinances, abandoned their evil practices and become remarkable for their diligence in the use of the means of grace?*

Answer: The previous character of those who seem to have been converted was varied. I could name quite a few in the higher ranks of life that seem evidently to have become new creatures who previously lived a worldly life, though unmarked by open wickedness. Many, again, who were nominal Christians before are now true believers. I could name, however, far more who have been turned from the paths of open sin and rebellion and have found pardon and purity in the blood of the Lamb and by the Spirit of our God; so that we can say to them, as Paul said to the Corinthians, "Such were some of you; but ye are washed, but ye are sanctified, but ye are justified." I often think, when conversing with some of these, that the change they have undergone might be enough to convince an atheist that there is a God, or an infidel that there is a Savior.

4. *Could you reveal the number of such cases?*

Answer: It is not easy for a minister in a field like this to keep an exact account of all the cases of awakening and conversion that occur, and there are many of which he may never hear. I have always tried to mark down the circumstances of each awakened soul that has come to me, and the number of these from first to last has been very great. During the autumn of 1839, no fewer than six to seven hundred came to converse with the ministers about their souls; and there were many more, equally concerned, who never came forward in this way. I know many who appear to have been converted, and yet have never come to me in private; and I am every now and then hearing of conversions of which I was not before aware. Indeed, eternity alone will reveal the true number of the Lord's hidden ones among us.

5. *Has the conduct of any of the parties been consistent, and if so, for how long?*

Answer: With regard to the consistency of those who are believed to have been converted, I may first of all remark that it must be acknowledged and should be clearly understood that many who came under concern for their souls, and seemed for a short time to be deeply convinced of sin, have gone back to the world. I believe at that remarkable season in 1839, there were very few persons who attended the meetings without being more or less affected. It pleased God at that time to bring a truly solemn sense of holy things over the minds of men. It was, indeed, the day of our merciful visitation. But many allowed it to slip past them without being saved; and these have fallen back, as must be expected, into their former deadness and impenitence. Alas, there are some among us whose very look reminds us of that awful warning, "Quench not the Spirit."

Confining our view, however, to those who, as far as ministers could judge by the rules of God's Word, seemed to be genuinely converted, I may with safety say that I do not know of more than two who have openly denied their profession. Other cases of this kind may have occurred, but they are unknown to me. More, I have no doubt, will eventually occur, for the voice of God teaches us to expect such things. Some of those converted have now walked consistently for four years; the greater part from one to two years. Some have had their falls into sin and have thus opened the mouths of their adversaries, but the very disturbance that this made shows that such instances are very rare. Some have fallen into spiritual darkness; many, I fear, have left their first love, yet I see nothing in all this but what is true in the case of every Christian church. There are many others who are filled with light and peace and are examples to believers in all things.

We had an additional Communion season at my return from the Continent that was the happiest and holiest at which I have ever been present. The Monday was entirely devoted to thanksgiving, and a thank-offering was made among us to God for His outstanding mercies. The times were hard, and my people are far from wealthy, yet the sum contributed was fifty dollars. This was devoted to missionary purposes. It is true that those whom I esteem as Christians do often grieve me by their inconsistencies; but still I cannot help thinking that if the world were full of such, the time would come when "they shall neither hurt nor destroy in all God's holy mountain."

6. *Have the means to which the revivals are ascribed been attended with beneficial results on the part of the people at large?*

Answer: During the progress of this work of God, not only have many individuals been genuinely converted but also important results have been produced upon the people in general. It is indeed amazing as well as truly disturbing to see that thousands living in the immediate vicinity of the spot where God has been dealing so graciously still continue in deep apathy with regard to spiritual things or are running headlong into open sin. While many from a distance have become heirs of glory, multitudes of those who live within the sound of the Sabbath bell continue to live in sin and misery. Still, however, the results felt by the community are very marked. It seems now to be agreed, even by the most ungodly, that there is such a thing as conversion. Indeed, men can no longer deny it.

The Sabbath is now observed with greater reverence than it used to be, and there seems to be on the minds of men a far more solemn awe than there was. I feel that I can stop sinners in the midst of their open sin and wickedness and command their reverent attention in a way that I could not have done before. The private meetings for prayer have spread a sweet influence. There is far more solemnity in the house of God, and the experience of preaching to the people is quite different now from what it once was. Any minister of spiritual discernment can sense that there are many praying people in the congregation. When I first came here, I found it impossible to establish Sunday schools within the local system, while recently there was instituted nineteen such schools that are well taught and well attended.

7. *Were there public manifestations or physical excitement, such as audible sobs, groans, cries, or screams in your revivals?*

8. *Did any of the parties throw themselves into unusual postures?*

9. *Were there any who fainted, fell into convulsions, or were ill in other respects?*

Answer: As I have already stated, by far the most remarkable season of the working of the Spirit of God in this place was in 1839, when I was abroad. At that time there were many seasons of remarkable solemnity, when the house of God literally became a Bochim ("a place of weepers"). Those who were privileged to be present at these times will, I believe, never forget them. Even since my return, I have frequently seen the preaching of the Word attended with much power, and eternal things brought so near that the emotions of the people could not be restrained. I have observed at such times an awesome and breathless stillness pervading the assembly; serious men covered their faces to pray that the arrows of the King of Zion might be sent home with power to the hearts of sinners.

Again, at such a time, I have heard a half-suppressed sigh rising from many a heart and have seen many bathed in tears. At other times I have heard loud sobbing in many parts of the church, while a deep solemnity pervaded the whole audience. I have also in some instances heard individuals cry aloud, as if they had been pierced through with a dart. These solemn scenes were witnessed under the preaching of different ministers, and sometimes occurred under the most tender gospel invitations. On one occasion, for instance, when the minister was speaking tenderly on the words "He is altogether lovely," almost every sentence was responded to by cries of bitterest agony. At such times I have seen persons so overcome that they could not walk or stand without assistance.

I have know cases in which believers have been similarly affected by the fullness of their joy. I have often known such awakenings to result in what I believe to be real conversion. I could name many of the humblest, meekest believers who at one time cried out in the church under deep agony. I have also met with instances where the sight of souls thus pierced has been blessed by God to awaken careless sinners who had come to mock.

I am far from believing that these sighs of deep alarm always issue in conversion, or that the Spirit of God does not often work in a quieter manner. Sometimes, I believe, He comes like the pouring rain; sometimes like the gentle dew. Still I would humbly state my conviction that it is the duty of all who seek the salvation of souls, and especially the duty of ministers, to long and pray for such solemn times, when the arrows shall be sharp in the heart of the King's enemies, and our slumbering congregations shall be made to cry out, "Men and brethren, what shall we do to be saved?"

10. *How late have you known revival meetings to last?*

11. *Do you approve or disapprove of these meetings on the whole? In either case, please state your reasons why.*

Answer: None of the ministers who have here engaged in the work of God have ever used the term "revival meeting," nor do they approve of its use. We are told in the book of Acts that the apostles preached and taught the gospel daily; yet their meetings are never called revival meetings. No other meetings have taken place here, but such as were held for the preaching and teaching of the gospel and for prayer. It will not be maintained by anyone that the meetings in the sanctuary every Lord's Day are intended for any other purpose than the revival of genuine godliness through the conversion of sinners and the edification of saints. All the meetings in this place were held, I believe, with a single eye to the same object. There seems, therefore, to be no purpose in applying the name particularly to any meetings that have been held in this place. It is true, indeed, that on weeknights there is not generally the same formality as on Sundays; the congregation is commonly dressed in their work clothes, and the minister speaks with less regular preparation.

During the autumn of 1839, the meetings were in general dismissed at ten o'clock, although in several instances the state of the congregation seemed to be such as to demand that the ministers remain still longer with them that they might counsel and pray with the awakened. I have once or twice seen the service in the house of God continue until about midnight. On these occasions the emotion during the preaching of the Word was so great that after the blessing had been pronounced at the usual hour, the greater part of the people remained in their seats or occupied the aisles, so that it was impossible to leave them. In consequence of this, a few words more were spoken suited to the state of awakened souls; singing and prayer filled up the rest of the time. In this way the meeting was prolonged by the very necessity of the situation.

On such occasions I have often longed that all the ministers in Scotland were present, that they might learn more deeply what the true end of our ministry is. I have never seen or heard of anything improper at such meetings, and on all such occasions the feelings that filled my soul were those of the most solemn awe, the deepest compassion for afflicted souls, and an unutterable sense of the hardness of my own heart. I do entirely and solemnly approve of such meetings, because I believe them to be in accordance with the Word of God, to be pervaded by the Spirit of Christ, and to be oftentimes the birthplace of precious, never-dying souls. It is my earnest prayer that we may yet see greater things than these in all parts of Scotland.

12. *Was there ever a death caused or said to be caused by over-excitement in any such meeting? If so, state the circumstances, insofar as you know them.*

Answer: There was one death that took place in very solemn circumstances at the time of the work of God in this place, and it was ascribed by many to the enemies of religious excitement. The facts of the case, however, which were published at the time, clearly showed that it was a groundless tale.

13. *State any other circumstances connected with revivals in*

your parish or district which, though not involved in the foregoing queries, may tend to throw light upon the subject.

Answer: I have been led to examine with particular care the accounts that have been left us of the Lord's marvelous works in the days that are past, both in our own land and in other parts of the world, in order that I might compare these with what has lately taken place in Dundee, and in other parts of Scotland. In doing this, I have been fully convinced that the outpouring of the Holy Spirit at the Shotts church, and under the ministry of Jonathan Edwards in America, was attended by the very same appearances as the work in our own day. Indeed, so completely do they seem to agree, both in their nature and in the circumstances that attended them, that I have not heard a single objection brought against the work of God now that was not brought against it in former times and that has not been most triumphantly removed by Jonathan Edwards in his invaluable *Thoughts on the Revival of Religion in New England*: "And certainly we must throw out all talk of conversion and Christian experience; and not only so, but we must throw out our Bibles, and give up revealed religion, if this is not in general the work of God."

14. *What special circumstances in the preaching or ministry of God's servants appear to have produced the results in each particular case that may have come under your notice?*

Answer: I am not aware of anything in the ministry of those who have occupied my pulpit that could be called peculiar, or in any way different from what I believe ought to characterize the services of all true ministers of Christ. They have preached, so far as I can judge, nothing but the pure gospel of the grace of God. They have done this fully, clearly, solemnly, and with discrimination, urgency, and love. I know that none of them simply read their sermons.

I believe they all seek the genuine conversion of their people, and they believe that under a living gospel ministry, success is the rule and lack of success the exception. They are, in general, particularly given to private prayer, and they have also been accustomed to having times of corporate prayer, especially before and after public worship. Some of them have been led to declare the judgments of the Lord, and others to set forth the fullness and freeness of Christ as the Savior of sinners; and of course the same persons have been at different times moved to preach on both of these subjects. So far as I am aware, no unscriptural doctrines have been taught, nor has there been a holding back of any part of "the whole counsel of God."

15. *Did these servants of God referred to also address children in special meetings? What were the times of these meetings, and what ages were taught?*

Answer: The ministers engaged in the work of God in this place, believing that children of accountable age are lost and may through grace be saved, have therefore spoken to children as freely as to grown-ups; and God has so greatly honored their labors that many children, from ten years old and up, have given full evidence of their being born again. I am not aware of any special meetings that have been held particularly for children, with the exception of the Sunday schools, the children's prayer meetings, and a sermon to children on the Monday evening after Communion. It was commonly at the public meetings in the house of God that children were convicted, and often also in their own classes, when no minister was present.

The "excesses" of revival are grossly exaggerated by the enemies of the gospel, those who can become excited about politics or sports but not about their soul's salvation. Emotional expression of penitence with tears or the joy of sins forgiven is not to be feared by true believers who are filled with the Spirit. Revival is the divine means for quickening or strengthening God's work in the world. We hold with Finney that revival is *"the only possible thing that can wipe away the reproach that covers the church, and restore religion to the place it ought to have in the estimation of the public . . . [that it] is indispensable to avert the judgment of God from the church"* and that nothing else *"will restore Christian love and confidence among church members . . . [or] preserve the church from annihilation."* Christianity without revival quickly becomes lifeless and useless, and the *"evils that are sometimes complained of, when they are real, are incidental and of small importance when compared with the amount of good produced by revivals."*

False Comforts for Sinners?

Equally subtle against the success of a revival movement is the peril of superficiality. The hindrances may be overcome by Christian grace and graciousness, desire and devotion, and the hue and cry against methods and excesses may go unheeded or prove to be groundless, and yet the efforts for evangelism will go unrewarded if Christians give false comfort to sinners. Finney learned this danger in his long experience and gave earnest warning against any counsel or procedure that in actuality prevented the sinner from coming "just as he was" to the Savior:

1. *One of the ways in which people give false comfort to distressed sinners is by asking them, "What have you done? You are not so bad."* For instance, a mother will tell her son who is under conviction of sin what an obedient child he has always been, or how good and how kind he is, and she will beg him not to be so disturbed. Or a husband will tell his wife, or vice-versa, how good the other is, and ask, "What have you done?"

The fact is, no sinner ever had the idea that his sins were greater than they are, because no sinner ever had an adequate idea of how great a sinner he is. It is not possible that any man could live under the full sight of his sins. God in His mercy has spared all of us that sight that is more terrible than we can imagine. The sinner's guilt is much deeper and more damning than he thinks, and his danger is much greater than he thinks it is. To tell the most moral and naturally amiable person in the world that he is good enough or that he is not as bad as he thinks he is, is not giving him rational comfort but is deceiving him and ruining his soul. Let those who do it take care.

2. *Others tell awakened sinners that conversion is a progressive work, and in this way ease their anxiety.* When a man is distressed because he sees himself to be such a sinner and that unless he turns to God he will be damned, it is a great relief to have a friend tell him he can get better by degrees, and that he is coming along, little by little, toward salvation. The truth is, regeneration, or conversion, is *not* a progressive work. Rather, it is but the *beginning* of obedience to God. Is the beginning of a thing progressive? No. It is the first act of genuine obedience to God—the first voluntary action of the mind toward what God approves. That is conversion.

3. *Another way in which convicted sinners are deceived with false comfort is by being advised to dismiss the subject for the present time.* Men who are supposed to be wise in matters of spiritual counsel have sometimes assumed to be wiser than God when He is dealing with a sinner by His Spirit, endeavoring to bring him to a decision. They think God is crowding the person and that it is necessary for them to interfere. They will advise the person to take a ride or go visit with someone or engage in business or something that will relieve his mind a little, at least for the present. Such advice—if what is distressing the sinner is truly conviction of sin—is neither safe nor wise. The strivings of the Spirit to bring a sinner to himself will never hurt him, nor will it drive him crazy, as some suppose. (He may make himself deranged by resisting.) It is blasphemous to think that the blessed, wise, and benevolent Spirit of God would ever conduct himself with so little care as to derange and destroy the soul He came to sanctify and save. The proper course to take with a sinner when the striving of the Spirit throws him into distress is to *instruct* him, to clear up his views, correct his mistaken thinking, and make the way of salvation so plain that he can see it right before him. Remember that if an awakened sinner voluntarily dismisses the subject once, he probably will not take it up again.

4. *Sometimes an awakened sinner is comforted by being told that religion does not consist in feeling bad.* I once heard of a doctor of divinity giving an anxious sinner such counsel when he

was actually writhing under the arrows of the Almighty. He told him, "Religion is cheerful; religion is not gloomy, do not be distressed; be comforted, dismiss your fears, you should not feel so bad," and such like miserable comforts, when, in fact, the man had infinite reason to be distressed, for he was resisting the Holy Spirit and in danger of grieving Him away forever.

Oh, what a doctrine of devils to tell a rebel against heaven not to be distressed! What is all his distress but rebellion itself? He is not comforted because he refuses to be comforted. God is ready to comfort him. You need not think yourself to be more compassionate than God. He will fill the sinner with comfort in an instant—if he will submit.

5. *Whenever religion is clothed in mystery, it is calculated to give a sinner false comfort*. When a sinner is under conviction of sin, and someone clouds the issue by steering the mind and heart away from what is happening, he will feel relieved. The sinner's distress arises from the pressure of obligation to repent and yield himself to God. Enlighten him on this point, and if he will not yield, it will only increase his distress. But tell him that regeneration is all a mystery, something that cannot be understood—leaving him in a fog of darkness—and you relieve his anxiety. It is his clear understanding of the nature and duty of repentance that produces his distress.

6. *Whatever relieves the sinner of his full sense of blame will give him false comfort*. The more a man feels himself to blame, the deeper his distress. So of course anything that lessens this sense of blame will also lessen his distress. However, it is a comfort that is short-lived. To deny blame is to deny guilt, and without a sense of guilt a man will not repent and be forgiven.

7. *To tell him he is incapable of repenting is also a false comfort*. To say to a convicted sinner, "What can you do? You are a poor, feeble creature; you can do nothing," will bring at first a kind of despondency. But it is not the keen remorse that brings him to repentance.

8. *If a sinner gets the idea that he is to be passive in his search,*

he will be falsely consoled. Give him the impression that he has nothing to do but to wait God's time and that conversion is the work of God and he ought to leave it to Him, and he will infer, as before, that he is not to blame and will feel immensely relieved. If he is only to remain still and let God do the work, he feels no responsibility at all. But such instruction is wrong. A sinner must own his responsibility to repent of sin and give himself up to God so that God can do His work of redemption.

9. *Telling a sinner to wait God's time is incomplete instruction*. Here stands a sinner in rebellion. God comes to him with pardon in one hand and a sword in the other, and tells him to repent and receive pardon or refuse and perish. Then comes a minister of the gospel who tells the sinner to wait for God's time. Virtually he is saying that God is not ready to have him repent just now, is not ready to pardon him now. If this is the case, the sinner can throw the blame of his impenitence upon God.

I have often thought such teachers need the rebuke Elijah gave when he met the priests of Baal: "Shout louder! . . . Surely he is a god! Perhaps he is deep in thought, or busy, or traveling. Maybe he is sleeping and must be awakened." The minister who ventures to intimate that God is not ready and who tells the sinner to await God's time, might as well tell him that God is traveling or asleep and cannot attend him at present. Miserable comforters, indeed! It is a little less than outrageous blasphemy. How many will stand at the Judgment seat of Christ with blood on their hands of the souls whom they have deceived and destroyed by telling them God was not ready to save them?

10. *It is false comfort to tell a convicted sinner to do anything for relief that he can do and yet not submit his heart to God*. An anxious sinner is often willing to do anything but the very thing that God requires him to do. He is willing to go to the ends of the earth or to pay a huge debt or to endure suffering or anything but full and instantaneous submission to God. Now, if you will compromise the matter with him and tell him of something else that he may do and yet evade that point, he will be very much com-

forted. He will like that instruction. He will say, "Oh, yes, I will do that; I like that minister, he is not so severe as the others. He seems to understand my particular situation, and knows how to make allowances." I will mention a few of the things sinners are told to do:

(a) *Use what means you have to do better*. Nothing he does can take the place of true repentance and faith in God's work of redemption. He can't *do* anything else.

(b) *Pray for a new heart*. God does not tell us to pray for a new heart. Rather, He gives us a new heart when we repent and submit to God. The psalmist prayed, "Create in me a clean heart, and renew a right spirit within me." But this attitude is far different than the sinner asking God to do what he must do himself. The psalmist's words suggest a penitent heart asking for cleansing and renewal.

(c) *Simply persevere*. Persevere in what? In struggling against God? That is just the instruction the devil would give. He wants us to persevere in the way we have been going and nothing more.

(d) *Press forward*. This is on the supposition that his face is toward heaven, when, in fact, his face may be toward hell and destruction if he is resisting the Holy Spirit. What should be told a sinner is, "Stop! Do not take another step in that direction. Turn toward God."

(e) *Try to repent and give your heart to God*. Giving this direction implies that it is very difficult to repent, perhaps impossible, and that the best thing a sinner can do is to *try* to see whether or not he can do it. What is this but substituting your own commandment for God's? God requires nothing short of repentance.

(f) *Pray for repentance*. The sinner will gladly pray for repentance, assuming again that God will do the work instead of him. He must be made to understand that he must do his part and repent of his sins.

(g) *Pray for conviction or pray for the Holy Spirit*. If the sinner is already under conviction, which he likely is if he has come for prayer, to ask him to pray for conviction is only to delay his obligation to repent immediately. He will want more *time*. Anything that will defer the present pressure to deal with his sins and submit his heart to God will only comfort him, but not cause him to do what he must do.

11. *Do not be alarmed, because God is only trying your faith by putting you under this burden of sin.* This is to say that the impenitent sinner already has faith! This is most confusing. God is not teaching him a lesson in patience but rather is laboring to bring him to a place of repentance so He can fill his soul with the peace of heaven.

12. *Leave your conversion in God's hands.* That is the same as telling him that he need not be converted *now*. How absurd! As if God would convert a sinner with no yielding at all on his part. No. God has required of him a change of heart, a turning around, and forsaking his sin. Nothing short of this will save the sinner.

13. *Do not be discouraged.* They will tell him, "I was under conviction for many weeks (or months, or years) and have gone through all of this myself. After some time I found relief, and I do not doubt that you will find it too. Do not despair." This is equal to telling someone to take courage in his rebellion.

14. *I have faith to believe you will be converted.* You have faith to believe? You cannot believe for someone else. The very design and object of the Spirit of God is to tear away from the sinner his last vestige of hope while remaining in sin. He must first and foremost turn from his sins and then believe for his own salvation. It cannot be done for him.

15. *I will pray for you.* The danger here is in the sinner putting his hope in your prayers instead of trusting in Christ.

16. *I rejoice to see you in this state, and I hope you will be faithful and hold out.* What is that but rejoicing to see him in rebellion against God? For that is precisely the ground on which he stands. He is resisting conviction, and resisting conscience, and resisting the Holy Spirit. Instead of rejoicing, you ought to be distressed to see him resisting God. The longer he resists, the harder his heart will become.

17. *God will reward you.* Again, there is misunderstanding of the sinner's state. This is not a trial but conviction of the Holy Spirit designed to lead a man to repentance.

18. *You have not repented enough.* The truth is, he has not repented at all. God comforts the sinner as soon as he repents. If he is in agony of soul, he has not yet repented.

19. *If you are one of the elect, you will eventually be brought in.* I once heard of a case where a person under great distress of mind was sent to converse with a neighboring minister. They talked a long time. As the person got up to leave, the minister asked to send a word with him to his father. The minister quickly wrote the letter and handed it to the young man, forgetting to seal it. As the sinner was going home, he saw that the letter was unsealed, and he thought to himself that probably the minister had written something about him, so he opened it and read words to this effect: "Dear sir, I find your son under conviction and in great distress, and it was not easy to say anything to relieve him. But if he is one of the elect, he will surely be brought in." He intended the words to comfort the father, but they well nigh ruined the soul of the son, because he settled down to rest on the doctrine of election and his conviction was gone. Years later he was awakened again and converted, but only after a great struggle and not until that false impression was obliterated from his mind and he was made to see that if he did not repent he would be damned.

20. *You are in a very prosperous way.* The thing that the Holy Spirit wants to make the sinner feel is that all his ways are wrong, and that they lead to hell. And everyone is conspiring to give the opposite impression. The way is not prosperous until he repents.

21. *Here is a Scripture for you to help you in your distress. . . .* The Scripture promises that are quoted are those intended only for believers. Some examples are, "Blessed are they that mourn, for they shall be comforted"; "Seek and you shall find"; "Be not weary in well doing, for in due time you shall reap if you faint not." These only give a false hope because they do not apply to sinners.

22. *I will tell you my experience*. This can be dangerous in the sense that one may feel he must copy the experience of the other in order to be saved.

23. *God has begun a good work in you and He will carry it on*. The work that God continues is the work that begins with repentance. I have known parents to tell their children this as soon as they show signs of being spiritually awakened (but not repented). They give up all anxiety about them and settle down to thinking that God has begun a good work in their children and He will carry it through to completion. It would be just as rational for a farmer to say about his grain as soon as it came up out of the ground: "Well, God has begun a good work in my field, and He will carry it on."

24. *Well, since you are here, you must have given up your sins*. It must not be assumed that he has done any such thing. To go forward for prayer in a state of conviction or sorrow for sin does not mean everything has been done that must be done.

25. *Do what you can and God will do the rest*. With this, sinners often get the idea that they *have done* all they can, when, in fact, they have done nothing at all. They must be instructed to confess all sin and repent of it, giving themselves up completely to God.

26. *Be thankful for what you have, and hope for more*. This can be a confusing statement to the unsaved seeker. Should he be thankful that he has acknowledged his need of the Savior? Let him not think acknowledging his need means he has been saved. Should he be thankful for conviction of sin? Let him not confuse conviction with repentance.

To misdirect a passing motorist may produce serious consequences, inconveniences at least, but to misdirect a sinner seeking the way to God may cause him to miss heaven forever.

PART THREE

The Message

7

Finney the Preacher

Finney was not a pulpit orator. But he was one of the most effective revival preachers. From him one learns what true revival preaching is. His messages were pointed, dealing with the intellect and the conscience, with the design to convince the sinner of his need of the Savior and of the sufficiency of the salvation offered to him. With singleness of purpose, Finney spoke to the lost. He was deliberate and plainspoken, perhaps colloquial, but never coarse or vulgar. He adopted no "ministerial tone" but was conversational in his presentation, with illustrations drawn from everyday life. His usual method of sermonizing was topical, and after announcing a single great spiritual truth to be found in a Scripture verse, he would proceed to analyze and explain the truth found there. He had a very thorough understanding of human nature and of the Word of God, and he had an unusual faculty for causing the Word of God to penetrate into the innermost recesses of the human heart. He believed that a preacher should be repetitious, approaching a given truth first from one angle and then another until there was no refuge left for the sinner. He spoke with directness and depth of feeling, with "great searching eyes" that seemed to peer into the innermost depths of his listeners.

He was an extemporaneous preacher, and in that regard was quite a pioneer in a day when the clergy were inclined to compose oratorical messages with frequent classical illustrations and then to read the sermons with unrelieved monotony. He believed strongly that after much prayer and study the preacher should pour out his heart to the people with confidence in the anointing of God's Spirit. While he himself was the object of much controversy, he did not believe that revival preaching should raise controversial subjects, lest the hearers be drawn to speculation and away from the Savior.

He was ever a lawyer in the pulpit. Trained in the exacting logic of law, he held that the gospel should be presented to his hearers clearly and fully, with reason rather than with dogma. Anticipating the objections of sinners, he proceeded to annihilate one by one their excuses for not coming to God. It was his custom to announce the outline of his message after giving the text, and then to expand the outline in logical procedure. Usually he concluded with observations of a very practical and pointed nature and an exhortation to immediate action on the part of the sinner. A Manchester, England, newspaper records for us the observations of an English journalist on the revival ministry of Finney when in the British Isles:

> Mr. Finney is well known in America and England. His preaching is marked by strong peculiarities. It is highly argumentative—keenly logical—yet, being composed of good, strong Saxon, is intelligible to the common people. Boldness, verging on severity, is one of its chief characteristics. Unpalatable truths are urged with a fearless courage. Human responsibility and the obligation of everyone to repent and believe the gospel are handled with a master's grasp. Professors are not suffered to hide beneath the covert of mere formalism or an orthodox creed. Masks, pretexts, subterfuges of all sorts, are exposed; and the selfish, the worldly, the cowardly, the in-

consistent, are driven from their retreats. Then comes the gospel, with its full and free antidote to despair; its gracious invitation to the penitent; its pardon and peace for the believing.

As to the content of his message, Finney presented the truth of God as he saw it. To the point of view of many, his theology may have been defective or partial at best, with its stress on the moral government of God in the affairs of man and the death of Christ as the Savior's substitution in the place of the sinner. It is the old argument of Abelard versus Anselm. When Finney was converted, the two extremes of theology with which he became familiar were old school hyper-Calvinism, stressing a limited atonement for an elect few, and Universalism, asserting the ultimate salvation of all. Finney believed the Bible taught that Christ in His atonement merely did that which was necessary as a condition of the forgiveness of sins, and not that which cancelled sin, in the sense of literally paying the indebtedness of sinners. Divine influence on mankind was moral not physical, providing a way of salvation from the penalty of sin and its power, but not by paying an exact price in substitution.

Finney and Jonathan Edwards would not have been in agreement as theologians but certainly were one in evangelistic appeal and effectiveness. Finney was very fond of quoting the works of Edwards, from which he had gleaned much spiritual help and impetus. By the same token, Edwards and his contemporary Wesley were not of one mind theologically, and Whitefield stood with Calvinistic Edwards against the Arminian position of Wesley; but all three were mightily used of God in bringing multitudes to saving faith in the Lord Jesus. Can it be that at the very best, our theology, like our knowledge, is limited because we are finite and not infinite, and that God uses the heart that is wholly and unreservedly dedicated to the Lord Jesus Christ and loves Him supremely? One reserves no place for heresy or ignorance, but have we reached the pinnacle of infinite understanding so that our theology is complete and conclusive?

As to content, Finney's messages were designedly doctrinal to inform his hearers of their desperate need for a Savior and God's provision of that Savior. His sermons were always practical, applying the theory of the doctrine expounded so as to make the message perfectly plain and understandable. There was a very strong ethical content to his messages, planned to speak to the conscience of his listeners and to convince the sinner of his lost estate by his own standards as well as by the Word of God. In this respect, Finney has a particular contribution to revival preaching in our day. We have had more than a generation of evangelism with little or no ethic and, I am therefore convinced, with correspondingly little effectiveness. The moral and ethical content stand out in Finney's preaching, and his audience could not avoid the issues that he raised. He was a man of strong convictions as to moral issues and was fearless in the presentation of them. While he believed in salvation by grace through faith, he spoke often of the conduct of the individual as evidence of his need for salvation. He would not water down the gospel by reducing it to a pious formula, which if repeated gave the sinner, however anxious he might be, assurance of salvation. Firsthand possession of saving faith should be expressed in possession of new life. Conduct should be consistent with the claim of having passed from death unto life by faith in Christ.

In the next chapters are presented five of Finney's sermons given over a wide span of years. Of necessity the content has been reduced, and they have been edited for the modern reader, but we trust this has been done without robbing the evangelist of his argument and effectiveness. Three consecutive messages were chosen because they are representative of the manner in which Finney presented the truth and then gave an exhaustive analysis of error. The message on "Moral Insanity" is one of the most heart-searching and solemn statements of truth I have ever read.

By and large, I have been able to preserve Finney's usual presentation: the outline, the message proper, and then the summary, commonly called "Remarks."

Let Finney speak for himself, or more accurately, let him speak for the Savior.

Editor's Note: Finney's *Lectures to Professing Christians* was re-titled *Crystal Christianity: A Vital Guide to Personal Revival* (Springdale, Pa.: Whitaker House, 1986).

8

Where Sin Occurs God Cannot Wisely Prevent It

"It is impossible but that offenses come; but woe unto him through whom they come!"

Luke 17:1 (KJV)

An "offense" as used in this passage is an occasion of falling into sin. It is anything that causes another to sin and fall.

It is plain that the author of the offense in this passage is conceived of as *voluntary* and as *sinful* in his act, otherwise the affliction of God would not be denounced upon him.

Consequently, the passage assumes that this sin is in some sense necessary and unavoidable. What is true of *this sin* in this respect is true of all other sin. Indeed, any sin may become an *offense* in the sense of a temptation to others to sin, and therefore its necessity and unavoidableness would then be affirmed by this text.

The doctrine of this text, therefore, is that *sin*, under the government of God, *cannot be prevented*. I purpose to examine this doctrine to show that, nevertheless, sin is utterly inexcusable as to the sinner.

When we say it is impossible to prevent sin under the government of God, the statement still calls for another inquiry: Where does this impossibility lie? Is it on the part of the sinner or on the part of God? Which is true: that the sinner cannot possibly abstain from sin or that God cannot prevent his sinning?

The first supposition answers itself, for it could not be sin if it were utterly unavoidable. It might be the sinner's misfortune, but nothing would be more unjust than to impute it to him as his crime if it were unavoidable.

But we shall better understand where this impossibility does and must lie, if we first recall to mind some of the elementary principles of God's government.

Let us, then, consider that God's government over men is moral and is known to be such by every intelligent being. By the term *moral* I mean that it governs by motives and does not move by physical force. It adapts itself to mind not to matter. It contemplates mind as having intellect to understand truth, sensibility to appreciate its bearing upon happiness, conscience to judge the right, and a will to determine a course of voluntary action in view of God's claims. So God governs the mind. Not so does He govern matter. The physical universe is controlled by quite a different sort of agency. God does not move planets in their orbits by motives but by a physical agency.

You need to distinguish broadly between the influence of motive on the mind and of mechanical force upon matter. The former implies volition; the latter does not. The former is adapted to mind and has no adaptation to matter; the latter is equally adapted to matter but has no possible application to the mind. In God's government over the human mind, all is voluntary; nothing is coerced as by physical force. There can be no power in heaven or earth to coerce the will as matter is coerced. The nature of the mind forbids its possibility. And if it were possible, it would still be true that insofar as God should coerce the human will He would cease to govern morally.

Every moral agent in the universe knows that God has done the best He could do in regard to sin. Men know this truth so well they can never know it better. You may at some future day realize it more fully when you shall come to see its myriad illustrations drawn out before your eyes; but no demonstration can make its proof more perfect than it is to your own minds today.

Now, sin does, in fact, exist under God's government. For this sin, God either is or is not to blame. And every man knows that God is *not* to blame for this sin, for man's own nature affirms that He would prevent it if He wisely could. Certainly if He were able wisely to prevent sin in any case where it actually occurs, then not to do so nullifies all our conceptions of His goodness and wisdom. He would be the greatest sinner in the universe if with power and wisdom adequate to the prevention of sin He had failed to prevent it.

Let me also note that what God cannot do wisely He cannot (speaking morally) do at all. For He cannot act unwisely. He cannot do things that wisdom forbids. To do so would be to un-deify himself. The supposition would make Him cease to be perfect, and this is equivalent to ceasing to be God.

This is not conjecture but logical certainty. No truth can be more irresistibly and necessarily certain than this. I once heard a minister say in a sermon, "It is not irrational to suppose that in each case of sin, it occurs as it does because God cannot prevent it." After he retired from the pulpit, I said to him, "Why did you leave the matter so? You left your hearer to infer that perhaps it might be some other way; that this was only a possible theory, that some other theory was perhaps even more probable. Why did you not say, 'This theory is certain and must be true'?"

Again, sin is always committed against God and despite motives of infinitely greater weight than those that lead to sin. The very fact that his conscience condemns the sin is the sinner's own judgment on the question, proving that in his own view the motives to sin are infinitely contemptible when put on a scale and measured against the sin in question. Every sinner knows that sin is a willful abuse of his own powers as a moral agent—of those noblest powers of his being in view of the fact that he is made in the image of God.

What sinner ever supposed that God neglects to do anything He wisely can do to prevent sin? If this is not true, what is conscience but a lie and a delusion? Conscience always affirms that God is clear of all guilt in reference to sin. In every instance in which conscience condemns the sinner, it necessarily fully acquits God.

These remarks will suffice to show that sin in every instance of its commission is on the part of the sinner utterly inexcusable.

Next, we will look at some *objections*.

1. *If God is infinitely wise and good, why do we need to pray at all? If He will surely always do the best possible thing, and all the good He can do, why do we need to pray?*

I answer: Because His infinite goodness and wisdom ask us to. Who could ask a better reason than this? If you believe in His infinite wisdom and goodness and make this belief the basis of your objection, you will certainly, if honest, be satisfied with this answer.

But again, I answer: It might be wise and good for Him to do many things, if they are asked of Him in prayer, that He could not wisely do if unasked. You cannot, therefore, infer that prayer never changes the course that God voluntarily pursues.

2. Objecting again, you ask, *Why should we pray to God to prevent sin if He cannot prevent it?* If, under the circumstances in which sin exists, God cannot, as you hold, prevent sin, why go to Him in prayer to prevent it?

I answer: We pray for the very purpose of changing the circumstances. This is our object. And prayer does change the circumstances. If we step forward and offer fervent, effectual prayer, this changes the state of the case.

3. Yet further objecting, you ask, *Why did God create moral*

agents at all, if He foresaw that He could not prevent their sinning?

I answer: Because He saw that on the whole it was better to do so. He could prevent some sin in this race of moral agents; could overrule what He could not wisely prevent, so as to bring out of it a great deal of good, and so that in the long run he saw it better, with all the results before Him, to create than not to create; therefore, wisdom and love made it necessary that He should create. Having the power to create a race of moral beings—having also power to convert and save a vast multitude of them, and power also to overrule the sin he should not prevent so that it should evolve immense good, how could He keep from creating as He did?

4. *But if God cannot prevent sin will He not be unhappy?* No. He is entirely satisfied to do the best He can and accept the results.

5. But some will say, *Is this not limiting the Holy One of Israel?* No. It is not a proper limitation of God's power to say that He cannot do anything that is unwise. Nor do we limit His power when we say He cannot move the mind just as He moves a planet.

But you say, *Could not God prevent sin by annihilating each moral agent the instant before he would sin?* Doubtless He could; but we say if this were wise He would have done it. He has not done it, certainly not in all cases, and therefore it is not always wise.

You may say, *Let Him give more of His Holy Spirit.* My answer is that He does give all He can—wisely, under existing circumstances. To suppose He might give more than He does, all things being the same, is to impeach His wisdom or His goodness.

Some are shocked at the idea of setting limits on God's power. Yet they make assumptions that inevitably impeach His wisdom and His goodness. Such persons need to consider that if we must choose between limiting His power on the one hand or His wisdom and His love on the other, it is infinitely more honorable to Him to adopt the former alternative than the latter. To strike a blow at His moral attributes is to annihilate His throne. Let it be also considered, as we have already suggested, that you do not in any offensive sense limit His power when you assume that he cannot do things naturally impossible and cannot act unwisely.

Remarks

1. We may see the only sense in which God could have purposed the existence of sin. It is simply negative. He purposed not to prevent it in any case where it does actually occur. He does not purpose to *make* moral agents sin—not, for example, Adam and Eve in the Garden, or Judas in the matter of betraying Christ. All He purposed to do himself was to leave them with only a certain amount of restraint—as much as He could wisely impose; and then if they would sin, let them bear the responsibility. He left them to act freely and did not positively prevent their sinning. He never uses means to make men sin. He only keeps from using unwise means to prevent their sinning. Thus His agency in the existence of sin is only negative.

2. The existence of sin does not prove that it is the necessary means of the greatest good. Some of you are aware that this point has been often mooted in theological discussions. I do not purpose now to go into it at length but will only say that in all cases wherein men sin they *could* obey God instead of sinning. Now, the question here is if they were to obey rather than sin would not a greater good accrue? We have these two reasons for the affirmative: (1) By natural tendency obedience promotes good and disobedience promotes evil, and (2) In all those cases God earnestly and positively urges obedience. It is fair to presume that He would desire that which would secure the greatest good.

3. The human conscience always justifies God. This is an undeniable fact—a fact of universal consciousness. The proof of it can never be made stronger, for it stands recorded in each man's heart.

The fact is, conscience always condemns the sinner and justifies God. It could not affirm obligation without justifying God. The real controversy, therefore, is not between God and the conscience, but between God and the *heart*. In every instance in which sin exists, conscience condemns the sinner and justifies God.

4. Conversion consists precisely in this: the heart's consent to these decisions of the conscience. It is for the heart to come over to the ground occupied by the conscience, and thoroughly acquiesce in it as right and true. Conscience has been speaking for a long time; it has always held one doctrine and has long been resisted by the heart. Now in conversion, the heart comes over and gives its full assent to the decisions of conscience: that God is right and that sin and the sinner are utterly wrong.

5. In the light of this subject, we can see the reason for a general judgment. God intends to clear himself before the entire moral universe from all imputation of wrong in the matter of sin. Strange facts have transpired in His universe, and strange insinuations have been made against His course. These matters must all be set aright. For this He will take time enough. He will wait until all things are ready. Obviously, He could not bring about His great Judgment Day until the deeds of earth have all been wrought—until all the events of this wondrous drama have been played out in full. Until then He will not be ready to make a full exposé of all His doings. *Then* He can and will do it most triumphantly and gloriously.

The revelations of that day will doubtless show why God did not interpose to prevent every sin in the universe. Then He will satisfy us as to the reasons He had for suffering Adam and Eve to sin and for allowing Judas to betray his Master. We know now that He is wise and good, although we do not know all the particular reasons for His conduct in the permission of sin. Then He will reveal those particular reasons, as far as it may be best and possible. No doubt He will then show that His reasons were so wise and good that He could not have done better.

6. Sin will then appear infinitely inexcusable and detestable. It will then be seen in its true relationship to God and His intelligent creatures—inexpressibly blameworthy and guilty.

7. God's omnipotence is no guarantee to any man that either he or any other sinner will be saved. I know the Universalist affirms it to be so. He will ask, *Does not the fact of God's omnipotence, taken in connection with His infinite love, prove that all men will be saved?* I answer, *No!* It does not prove that God will save one soul. With ever so much proof of God's perfect wisdom, love, and power, we could not infer that he would save even one sinner. We might just as reasonably infer that He would send the whole race to hell. How could we know what His wisdom would determine? Our knowledge is wholly from revelation. *God has said so*; and this is all we know about it.

Yet further I reply to the Universalist that God's omnipotence saves nobody. Salvation is not wrought by physical omnipotence. It is only by moral power that God saves, and this can save no man unless he consents to be saved.

8. How bitter the reflections that sinners must have on their deathbed, and how fearfully agonizing when they pass behind the veil and see things in their true light. Did you ever think when you have seen a sinner dying in his sins what an awful thing it is for a sinner to die? You mark the lines of anguish on his countenance; you see the look of despair; you observe he cannot bear to hear a word about his awful future. There he lies, and death pushes on its stern assault. And where is he now? Not beyond the scope of thought and reflection. He can see back into the world he has left. He can still *think*. Alas, his misery is that he can do nothing *but* think! As said the prisoner in his solitary cell: "I could bear torture or I could endure toil; but oh, to have nothing to do but to *think*! To hear the voice of friend no more—to say not a word—to do nothing from day to day and from year to year but to *think*—that is awful." So it is with the lost sinner. Who can measure the misery of incessant, self-agonizing thought? God tried in vain to bless and save you. You fought Him and brought down on your guilty head a fearful *damnation*.

9. What infinite consolation will remain to God after He shall have closed up the entire scene of earth! He has banished the

wicked and taken home the righteous to His bosom of love and peace. I have done, says He, all I wisely could to save the race of man. I made sacrifices cheerfully, sent my well-beloved Son gladly, waited as long as it seemed wise to wait, and now it only remains to overrule all this pain and sorrow for the utmost good, and rejoice in the bliss of the redeemed forevermore.

There are the guilty lost. Their groans rise and echo up the walls of their pit of sorrow; it is to the holy so much evidence that God is good and wise and will surely sustain His throne in equity and righteousness forever. It teaches most impressive lessons upon the awful condemnation of sin. There let it stand and bear its testimony, to warn other beings against a course so reprehensible and a fate so dreadful!

There in that world of care may be some of our pupils, possibly some of our own children. But God is just and His throne stainless of their blood. It shall not mar the eternal joy of His kingdom that they would pull down such damnation on their heads. They insisted they would take the responsibility, and now they have it.

Sinner, do you not care about this today? Will you come to the inquiry meeting this evening to trifle about your salvation? I can tell you where you will not trifle. When the great bell of time shall toll the death knell of earth and call her millions of sons and daughters to the final Judgment. You will not then be in a mood to trifle! And you will surely be there. It will be a time for serious thought—an awful time of dread. Are you ready to face its revelations and decisions?

Or do you say, *"Enough, enough!* I have long enough withstood His grace and spurned His love; I will now give my heart to God, to be His only, forevermore"?

9

Moral Insanity

"The hearts of men, moreover, are full of evil and there is madness in their hearts while they live."

Ecclesiastes 9:3

The Bible often ascribes to unconverted men one common heart or disposition. It always makes two classes, and only two, of our race—saints and sinners—the one class converted from their sin and become God's real friends, the other remaining His unconverted enemies. According to the Bible, therefore, the heart is the same in its general character in all unregenerated men. In the days of Noah, God testified "how great man's wickedness on the earth had become, and that every inclination of the thoughts of his heart was only evil all the time" (Genesis 6:5). Observe that He speaks of the thoughts of *their heart* as if they had one common heart—all alike in moral character. So by Paul, God testifies that "the sinful mind is hostile to God" (Romans 8:7), speaking thus not of one man or of a few men, but of all men of carnal [sinful] mind. So in our text, the phraseology is expressive: "The hearts of men are full of evil"—as if men had but one heart—all in common—and this one heart were "full of evil." You will notice this

185

affirmation is not made of one or two men or of *some* men merely, but "of men," as if of them all.

1. But what is intended by affirming that "there is *madness* in their heart while they live"?

This is not the madness of anger but of insanity. True, sometimes people are mad with anger; but this is not the sense of our text. The Bible, as well as customary speech, employs the term "madness" to express *insanity*. This we understand to be its sense here.

Insanity is of two kinds—one of the head, the other of the heart. In the former, the intellect is disordered; in the latter, it is the *will* and voluntary powers that are affected. Intellectual insanity destroys moral agency. The intellectually insane is not, for the time, a moral agent; moral responsibility is suspended because he cannot *know* his duty and cannot choose responsibility as to doing or not doing it. True, when a man makes himself temporarily insane, as by drunkenness, the courts are obliged to hold him responsible for his acts committed in that state; but the guilt really belongs to the voluntary act that created the insanity.

The general law is that while the intellect retains its usual power the moral obligation remains unimpaired. Moral insanity, on the other hand, is *will* madness. The man retains his intellectual powers unimpaired, but he sets his heart to do evil. He refuses to yield to the demands of his conscience; he practically discards the obligations of moral responsibility. He has the powers of free moral agency but persistently abuses them. He has a reason that affirms obligation, but he refuses obedience to its affirmations.

In this form of insanity, the reason remains unimpaired but the heart deliberately disobeys.

The insanity spoken of in the text is *moral*, that of the *heart*. By the heart here is meant the will—the voluntary power. While the man is intellectually *sane*, he acts as if he were intellectually *insane*.

2. It is important to point out some of the manifestations of

this state of mind. Since the Bible affirms it to be a fact that sinners are mad in heart, we may naturally expect to see some manifestations of it. It is often striking to see how perfectly the Bible depicts human character; has it done so in reference to this point? We will see.

Who are the *morally insane*?

Those who are not *intellectually insane* act as if they are.

For example, those who are intellectually insane treat fiction as if it were reality and reality as if it were fiction. They also act as if *self* were of supreme importance and everything else of relatively no importance. Suppose you were to see a man acting this out in everyday life. Note that while wicked men talk as if they know better, yet they act as if all this were true—as if they really thought their own self-interest was more important than everything else in the universe, and as though God's interests, even His rights, were nothing in comparison. Practically every sinner does this. It is an essential element in all sin. Selfish men never regard the rights of anyone else unless they are in some way linked with their own.

If wicked men really believed their own rights and interests to be supreme in the universe, it would prove them intellectually insane, and we should hasten to send them away to the nearest mental institution; but when they show that they know better, and yet act on this groundless assumption in the face of their better knowledge, we say with the Bible that "there is madness in their hearts while they live."

Again, see this madness manifested in his relative estimate of time and eternity. His whole life declares that in his view it is by far more important to secure the good of time than the good of eternity. Yet if a man should *reason* thus—should argue to prove it and soberly assert it—you would know him to be insane. But suppose he does not *say* this—dares not say it—knows it is not true, yet constantly acts it out and lives on the assumption of its truth, what then? Simply this—he is morally mad. There is madness in his *heart*.

Now, this is precisely the practice of everyone who is living in sin. They give preference to time over eternity. They say in essence, "Oh give me the joys of time, why should I trouble myself yet about the trivial matters of eternity?"

In the same spirit, they assume the body is more than the soul. But if a man were to actually affirm this and go around trying to prove it, you would know him to be insane. And if he were a friend of yours, how your heart would break at his sad misfortune—his reason lost! But if he knows better, yet practically lives as if it were so, you say, "He is *merely* morally insane!"

Suppose you were to see a man destroying his own property—not by accident or mistake but deliberately; injuring his own health also, as if he had no care for his own interests. You might bring his case before a judge and declare a commission of lunacy against him, under which the man's goods should be taken out of his own control and he be no longer allowed to squander them. Yet in spiritual things, wicked men will deliberately act against their own best interests. Having a way put into their hands to get wisdom, they will not use it; having the treasures of heaven placed within reach, they do not try to secure them; with an infinite wealth of blessedness proffered for the mere acceptance of it, they will not take it as a gift. Indeed, in moral questions, wicked men seem to take the utmost pains to subvert their own interests and make themselves insolvent forever! Oh, how they rob their souls when they might have the riches of heaven!

Again, they endeavor to realize obvious impossibilities. For example, they try to make themselves happy in their sins and their selfishness, even though they know they cannot do it. Ask them, and they will admit that it is utterly impossible; and yet despite this conviction, they keep up the effort—as if they expected to eventually realize the impossibility. Now, in moral things it may not strike you as especially strange, for it is exceedingly common, but suppose in matters of the world you were to see a man doing the same sort of thing. What would you think of him? Men as surely know that they cannot obtain happiness in sin and selfishness as they know they cannot ensure health and comfort by mutilating their own flesh and inflicting harm upon their bodies. Doing consistently what they know will always defeat and never ensure real happiness, they show themselves to be morally insane.

Another manifestation of intellectual insanity is loss of confidence in one's best friends. Often this is one of the first and most painful evidences of insanity—the poor man will be convinced that his dearest friends are determined to ruin him. By no amount of evidence can he be persuaded to think they are his true friends.

In the same way sinners in their madness treat God. While they inwardly know He is their Friend, in practice they treat Him as their worst enemy. By no motivation can they be persuaded to confide in Him as their Friend. In fact, they treat Him as if He were the greatest liar in the universe. Amazing as it may seem, they practically reverse the regard due respectively to God and to Satan—treating Satan as if he were God and God as if He were Satan. Satan they believe and obey; God they disown, dishonor, and disobey.

Everyone knows, if they stop to think about it, that they treat God in this way. They regard the service of God as if it were inconsistent with their true and highest happiness. I have often met with sinners who seemed to think that every attempt to make them Christians is a scheme to take them in and sell them into slavery. They by no means estimate a life of faith as if it came forth from a God of love. In practice, they treat religion as if it would be their ruin if it were embraced. In all this they act utterly against their own convictions. They *know* better. If they did not, their guilt would be very small compared with what it is.

Another remarkable manifestation of insanity is to be greatly agitated about trifles and apathetic about the most important matters in life. Suppose you see a man enthused about straws and pebbles—taking unwearied pains to gather them into heaps and store them away as treasures; yet when a fire breaks out around his dwelling and the village is in flames, he takes no notice of it and feels no keen interest in it. People may die on every side of him with the plague, but he takes no heed to it. Would you not say he must be insane? But this is precisely true of sinners. They are infinitely taken up with worldly goods—straws and pebbles, compared with God's proffered treasures—but apathetic about the most momentous events on this earth.

The conduct of impenitent men is the perfection of irrationality. When you see it, you will get a more accurate and vivid idea of irrationality than you can get from any other source. You can see it in the ends to which they devote themselves and in the means that they employ to secure them. All is utterly unreasonable. An end madly chosen, sought by means madly devised—this is the life history of the masses that reject God. If this were the result of wrong intellectual judgments, we would say at once that the race has gone mad.

Sinners act as if they are afraid they might be saved. At least they seem to be trying to make their salvation as difficult as possible: they regard damnation as if it were salvation and salvation as if it were damnation. They rush upon damnation as if it were heaven and flee salvation as if it were hell.

Is this an exaggeration? I don't think so. This is only the simple truth. Sinners press down the way to hell as if it were the chief aim of their existence, and shun the way to heaven as if it were the consummation of evil. Sinner, this is your true moral state. The picture gives only the naked facts of the case, and I think without exaggeration.

3. This moral insanity is a state of unadulterated wickedness. The special quality of it that makes it a guilty state is that it is altogether *voluntary*. It is not the result of *loss* of reason but the *abuse* of reason. The will persists in acting against reason and conscience. Despite the affirmations of reason and regardless of the admonitions of conscience, the sinner presses on in his life of rebellion against God and goodness. In such voluntary waywardness is there not intrinsic guilt?

His actions, being deliberate, mean the man sins by willful choice as well as in thoughtless spontaneity. If he sins overtly and boldly, he is not apt to repent and change his position toward God in his quieter moments of rational thought, but virtually endorses the hasty actions of his careless hours. This, of course, heightens his guilt.

Again, his purposes of sin are obstinate and unyielding. In a thousand ways God is bringing influences to bear on his mind to change his purposes, but this is usually in vain. His life of sin is in violation of all known responsibilities. The sinner never acts from right motives, never yields to the sway of a sense of obligation, never recognizes his duty to love his neighbor as himself or to honor the Lord his God.

It is a complete rejection of both God's law and the gospel. The law he will not obey, the gospel of pardon he will not accept. He seems determined to brave the omnipotence of God and dare His vengeance. Is the Bible saying too much when it affirms, "There is madness in their hearts while they live"?

Remarks

1. Sinners strangely accuse saints of being crazy. Just as soon as Christians begin to act as if the truth they believe is a reality, wicked men cry out, "See, they are going crazy!" Yet these very sinners admit the Bible to be true and the things that Christians believe to be true as well, and further they admit that those Christians are doing only what they ought to do; and still they charge them with insanity. It is curious that even sinners know Christians to be the only rational beings on earth. I can well remember that I saw this plainly before my own conversion. I knew then that Christians were the only people in the world who had any valid claim to sanity.

2. If intellectual insanity is a shocking fact, how much more so is moral insanity? I have referred to my first impressions at the sight of one who was intellectually insane, but a case of moral insanity ought to be deemed far more astounding.

Think how horrible it would be to see a well-known intellectual lose his mental faculties and become insane. Then think how much worse if that same personality lost all moral principle and became a drunkard, a wife beater, a loafer; if this were to occur, we would be shocked and saddened and shake our heads in wonder. Intellectual idiocy is not to be compared to moral collapse.

3. Although some sinners may be externally fair and may seem to be amiable in temper and character, yet every real sinner is actually *insane*. In view of all the solemnities of eternity, he insists on being controlled by the things of time. With power to rise above, he does not even aim above the low pursuits of his selfish heart. With eternity so vast and its coming so certain, yet the sinner drives furiously on the road to hell as if he were on the highway to heaven—and all this because he is infatuated with the pleasures of sin for a season. At first glance, he seems to have made the mistake of hell for heaven, but on closer examination, you see it is not a mistake—he knows very well the difference, but he has deluded himself. The sad fact is that he *loves sin*, and after it he will go! So in a virtual state of insanity he rushes on to certain damnation as though he were in pursuit of heaven!

We shudder at the thought of any of our friends becoming mentally ill, but this would not be half so bad as to have one of them become wicked. Better to have a whole family lose their mental capacities than for one of them to become a hardened sinner. Indeed, the former compared with the latter is as nothing. For the mentally insane shall not always be so. When this mortal is laid away in the grave, the soul may look out again in the free air of liberty as if it had never been trapped in a dark prison; and the body, raised again, may bloom in eternal vigor and beauty; but moral insanity only waxes worse and worse forever—the root of it being not in a diseased brain but in a diseased heart and soul. Death cannot cure it; the resurrection will only raise him to shame and everlasting contempt.

Conversion to God is equal to becoming morally *sane*. It consists in restoring the will and the affections to the control of the intelligence, the reason, and the conscience, so as to put the man once more in harmony with himself—all his faculties adjusted to their true positions and proper functions.

Sometimes persons who have become converted but not well established, backslide into moral insanity. Just as persons sometimes relapse into intellectual insanity after being apparently restored. The latter is a sad situation and brings sorrow to the hearts of family and friends. But in no way can it be so sad as a case of backsliding into moral insanity.

Oh sinner, take care that you do not put out the light that God has cast into your dark heart, lest when you pass away it shall grow darker still and open into darkness forever.

10

True Saints

"Who is on the Lord's side?"

Exodus 32:26 (KJV)

The question was addressed by Moses to the professed people of God immediately after their great departure from God while Moses was on the Mount, when they worshiped a golden calf that had been cast for them by Aaron. After remonstrating with the guilty nation, he called out, "Who is on the Lord's side?" It is not my intention to dwell on the history of this particular case but to come to the point of my talk, which is to show that there are three classes of professing Christians:

1. the true friends of God and man
2. those who are motivated by hope and fear, or in other words by self-love or by selfishness
3. those who are motivated by public opinion

These three classes may be identified by looking at the characteristic developments that show the main purpose of their religion. It need not be proven that persons may start out from very different motives—some out of real love and some for other reasons. The differences may be arranged in these three classes, and by attending to the development of their true purpose in becoming Christians one learns their character.

I will proceed to list the characteristics of those who make up the first class—those who are the true friends of God and man.

1. *They are truly and sincerely benevolent.* They will make it plain that this is their character by their careful avoidance of sin. They will show that they hate it in themselves and that they hate it in others. They will not justify it in themselves and they will not justify it in others. They will not seek to cover up or to excuse their own sins, and neither will they try to cover up or to excuse the sins of others. In short, they aim at *holiness*. This course of conduct makes it evident that they are the true friends of God. I do not mean to say that every truly affectionate and obedient child is perfect or that he never fails in duty to his parents. But if he is an affectionate and obedient child, his aim is to always obey, and if he fails in any respect he by no means justifies it, or pleads for it, or aims to cover it up, but as soon as he realizes it he is dissatisfied with himself and condemns his conduct.

2. *They manifest a deep abhorrence of the sins of other people.* They do not cover up the sins of others, or plead for them and excuse them, or smooth them over by "perhaps this" or "perhaps that." You never hear them apologizing for sin. As they are indignant at sin in themselves, they are as much so when they see it in others. They know its nature and abhor it always.

3. *They have a zeal for the honor and glory of God.* They show the same ardor to promote God's honor and interest that the true patriot does to promote the honor and interest of his country. If he greatly loves his country, its government, and its interest, he sets his heart upon promoting its advancement and benefit. He is never so happy as when he is doing something for the honor and advancement of his country.

There are multitudes of professing Christians, and even ministers, who are very zealous to defend their own character and their own honor. But this class feels more engaged, and their hearts beat faster when defending or advancing God's honor.

These are the friends of God and man.

4. *They show that they sympathize with God in His feelings toward man*. They have the same kind of friendship for souls that God feels. I do not mean that they feel in the same degree, but that they have the same kind of feelings. There is such a thing as loving the souls of men while hating their conduct.

There is another peculiar kind of sympathy that the true child of God feels and manifests toward sinners. It is a combined feeling of abhorrence and compassion, of indignation against his sins and pity for his person. It is possible to feel this deep abhorrence of sin mingled with deep compassion for souls capable of such endless happiness and yet bound to eternal misery.

There are two kinds of love. One is the love of benevolence. This has no respect to the character of the person loved, but merely views the individual as exposed to suffering and misery. This is the kind of love God feels toward all men. The other kind includes esteem or approbation of character. God feels this only toward the righteous. He never feels *this* kind of love toward sinners. He demonstrates an infinitely strong compassion and abhorrence at the same time. Christians have the same feelings but not in the same degree. Did you ever see a parent yearning with compassion over a child and yet reprove him soundly with tears? Jesus Christ often manifested strongly these two emotions. He wept over Jerusalem because they killed the prophets and stoned those who were sent to them. What a full view He had of their wickedness at the same moment that He wept with compassion for the doom that hung over them.

Remember this point: The true friend of God and man never takes the sinner's part, because he never acts through mere compassion. And at the same time, he is never seen to denounce the sinner without manifesting compassion for his soul and a strong desire to save him from death.

5. *Their strong desire is to make others the friends of God*. Whether they converse, or pray, or attend to the everyday duties

of life, it is their prominent object to recommend Jesus Christ and to lead everyone to glorify God.

If this is not the leading feature of your character, if it is not the absorbing topic of thought and effort to reconcile men to God, you do not have the root of the matter in you. Whatever appearance of religion you may have, you lack the leading and fundamental characteristic of true spirituality.

6. *They scrupulously avoid everything that in their estimation is calculated to defeat their great end.* Look at the temperance reformation for an illustration of this. It was this group of persons that saw the need to do something about that which could harm souls and lead them away from God. These do not say, "Drinking rum is nowhere prohibited in the Bible, and I do not feel bound to give it up." Rather, they find that it hinders the great object for which they live, and that is enough for them.

A person who is strongly desirous of the conversion of sinners does not need an express prohibition to prevent his doing that which he sees is calculated to prevent this. There is no danger of his doing that which will defeat the very object of his life.

7. *They are distressed when they do not see sinners being converted.* Such professors as these are a great trouble to those who are religious for other motives, and who therefore wish to keep all quiet and orderly and have everything go on as it always has. They are often called "uneasy spirits in the church." That is, the minister will be made uneasy unless his preaching is such as to convert sinners.

8. *They manifest a spirit of prayer, praying not for themselves but for sinners.* If you know the habitual tenor of people's prayers, it will show which way the tide of their feelings is set. If a man is motivated mainly by a desire to save himself, you will hear him praying chiefly for himself—that he may have his sins pardoned and that he may enjoy the Spirit of God and the like. But if he is truly the friend of God and man, you will know that the burden of his prayers is for the glory of God in the salvation of sinners, and he is never so copious and powerful in prayer as when he gets

on his favorite topic: the conversion of the lost.

9. *These persons do not ask what they are "required" to do for the conversion of sinners.* When anything is presented to them that promises success in converting sinners, they do not wait to be urged to do it. They only want the evidence that it is calculated to advance the object on which their hearts are set, and they will engage in it with all their soul.

10. *They have the disposition to deny themselves in order to do good to others.* God has established throughout the universe the principle of giving. Even in the natural world, the rivers, the ocean, the clouds, all give. It is so throughout the whole kingdom of nature and of grace. This diffusive principle is everywhere recognized. This is the very spirit of Christ. He sought not to please himself but to do good to others. He found his highest happiness in denying himself for the sake of others. So it is with this class of persons—they are ever ready to deny themselves of enjoyments and comforts and even of necessities, when by so doing they can do more good to others.

11. *They are continually devising new means and new measures for doing good.* Where an individual is aiming mainly at his own salvation, he may think if he does his duty he is discharged from responsibility, and so he is satisfied—he thinks he has escaped from divine wrath and gained heaven for himself by doing what God required him to do, and he cannot help it that sinners are saved or lost. But with the true believer, it is not so much their object to gain heaven and avoid wrath as to save souls and to honor God.

12. *They express great grief when they see the church asleep and doing nothing for the salvation of sinners.* They know the difficulty—the impossibility—of doing anything considerable for the salvation of sinners while the church is asleep. Those who have other objects in view in being religious may think they are doing very well without being grieved over a sleeping church.

13. *They are grieved if their minister does not reprove the church pointedly and faithfully for their sins.* The other classes of profes-

sors are willing to be rocked to sleep, and willing that their minister preach smooth, flowery, and eloquent sermons, even flattering sermons, with no point and no power. But the true followers are not satisfied unless he preaches powerfully and boldly, and rebukes and entreats and exhorts with all long-suffering and doctrine.

14. *These will always stand by a faithful minister who preaches the truth.* No matter if the truth he preaches strikes them with conviction, they will consider it faithful and needful. When the truth is poured forth with power, their souls are fed and grow stronger in grace. They pray for such a minister, while others may scold him and talk about his being too strict or particular.

15. *These Christians are especially distressed when ministers preach sermons not adapted to convert sinners or stir up believers.* Others may approve the sermon, even praise it, and tell how eloquent it was, or lucid, or grand, or sublime, but the true believer looks for the vital characteristic—a tendency to convert sinners.

16. *These will generally speak in terms of dissatisfaction with themselves that they do not do more for the conversion of sinners.* However much they may really "do" for this object, it seems that the more they do, the more they long to do. They are never satisfied. Instead of being satisfied with the present degree of their success, there is no end to their longing for the salvation of the lost.

17. *This group is moved most when the situation of sinners is addressed.* You will find this will move their souls and set them on fire sooner than any appeal to their own hopes or fears.

Do you belong to this class of Christians or not? Before God, do you have these characteristics of a child of God? Do you *know* they belong to you? Can you say, "Oh Lord, you know all things. You know that I love you, and that these are the features of my character"?

11

Legal Religion

We have mentioned the three classes of professors of religion: those who truly love God and man, those who are motivated solely by selfishness (or at most self-love) in their religious duties, and those who are motivated only by a regard for public opinion. Now I will list several characteristics of the second class.

I will show how those professors who are actuated by self-love or by selfishness reveal this by their conduct. The conduct of men invariably shows what is their true and main purpose.

In this class, hope and fear are the mainsprings of all they do in their practice of religion.

1. *They make religion a subordinate concern.* They show by their conduct that they do not regard religion as the principle business of life but as subordinate to other things. They make a distinction between religious duty and business and consider them as entirely separate concerns. Whereas if they had right views of the matter, they would consider religion as the *only* business of life and nothing else worth pursuing unless it promotes or serves religion.

2. *Their religious duties are performed as a task and are not the*

result of the constraining love of God that burns within them. Such a one does not delight in the exercise of religious disciplines, and as to communion with God, he knows nothing of it. He performs prayer as a task. He takes part in religious duties as sick persons take medicine, not because they love it but because they hope to derive some benefit from it.

3. *They manifestly possess a legal spirit and not a gospel spirit*. They do what they are obliged to do in religion and not what they love to do. They have an eye to the commands of God, and yield obedience to His requirements in performing religious duties, but do not engage in those things because they love them. They are always ready to inquire in regard to duty not so much how they can do good as how they can be spared effort. The principal object of such a professor of religion is not to save the world but to save himself.

4. *They are mobilized more by fear than by hope*. They perform their religious duties chiefly because they dare not omit them. They have the spirit of slaves, and go about the service of God as slaves go about the service of their master, feeling that they are obliged to do so much or be beaten. So these professors feel they are obliged to do so much or be lashed by conscience and lose all hope.

5. *Their religion is not only produced by the fear of disgrace or the fear of hell but also by the avoidance of negatives*. They satisfy themselves with doing nothing that is very bad. Having no spiritual views, they regard the law of God chiefly as a system of prohibitions to guard men from certain sins and not as a system of benevolence fulfilled by love. And so if they are moral in their conduct, tolerably serious and decent in their general deportment, and perform the required amount of religious exercises, they are satisfied.

6. *This class of persons is more or less strict in religious duties according to the light they have and the sharpness with which their conscience pursues them*. Where they have enlightened minds and tender consciences, you often find them the most rigid of all pro-

fessors. They are perfect Pharisees, and carry everything to the greatest extreme so far as outward strictness is concerned.

7. *They are more or less miserable in proportion to the tenderness of their conscience.* With all their strictness, they cannot realize that they are great sinners after all; and having no good sense of gospel justification, this leaves them very unhappy. And the more enlightened and tender their conscience, the more they are unhappy. Notwithstanding their strictness, they feel that they come short of their duty, and not having any gospel faith or any holy anointing of the Holy Spirit that brings peace to the soul, they are unsatisfied and uneasy and miserable.

8. *These persons are encouraged and cheered by reading the accounts of ancient saints who fell into great sins.* They feel wonderfully instructed and edified when they hear the sins of God's people set forth in a strong light. They feel oddly comforted and their hopes are strengthened. Instead of feeling humbled and distressed, they feel a certain gratification.

9. *They are pleased when a lower standard of spirituality is preached from the pulpit.* If the minister adopts a low standard, and is ready to charitably hope that almost everyone is a Christian, they are pleased and compliment him for his expansive goodwill and praise him as an excellent preacher.

10. *They are fond of having "comfortable" doctrine preached.* Such persons are apt to be fond of having the doctrine of the saints' perseverance much dwelt upon and the doctrine of election preached. Often they want nothing else but what they call the "doctrines of grace." And if these doctrines can be preached in such an abstract way as to afford them comfort without galling their consciences too much, they are fed.

11. *They love to have their ministers preach sermons "to feed Christians."* Their main object is not to save sinners but to be saved themselves, and therefore they always choose a minister not for his ability in preaching for the conversion of sinners but for his talents in feeding the church with mere abstractions.

12. *They lay great stress on having "a comfortable hope."* You

will hear them talking very solemnly about the importance of having a comfortable hope. If they can enjoy only their own comfort, they show very little anxiety whether anybody else around them is saved or not. If they can only have their fears silenced and their hopes cherished they have religion enough to satisfy them.

In stark contrast to this, you will find the true friends of God and man thinking mainly of pulling sinners out of the fire and not spending their energy in sustaining a comfortable hope for themselves.

13. *They live primarily by what they conjure up in their own minds of past blessings and experiences*. They lay great stress on the particular feelings they have had from time to time. It does not matter if they are not doing anything to serve God *now*, or even if they feel no love for God now, they simply recall the times when they did, and this keeps their hopes alive. If there has been a revival, and they mingled in its scenes until their imaginations were worked up so that they could weep and pray and exhort with feeling, that experience will last them a long time, and they will have a comfortable hope for years on the strength of it.

14. *They pray almost exclusively for themselves*. If you could listen in on their prayers, you would hear eight-tenths of all their petitions going up for themselves.

15. *Such persons pray to be fitted for death much more than for a useful life*. They are more anxious to be prepared to die than to warn sinners around them and to serve the body of Christ. An individual who makes it his absorbing objective to do good and to save sinners will not be apt to think so much about when or where or how he will die as how he may do the most good while he lives.

16. *They are more afraid of punishment than they are of sin*. These will indulge in sin if they think they can repent later and can persuade themselves that God will forgive them. In contrast, the true friend of God is not half so much afraid of hell as of committing sin.

17. *They feel and manifest greater anxiety about being saved*

themselves than if all the world were going to hell.

18. *They are more fond of receiving good than of doing good.* You may know such persons have not the spirit of the gospel. They have never entered into the spirit of Jesus Christ when He said, "It is more blessed to give than to receive." A person actuated by true love to God and man enjoys what he does to benefit others far more than the one who receives it.

19. *When this class of professors is asked to pray for the conversion and salvation of others, you will note that they are mobilized by the same considerations as when they pray for themselves.* They are chiefly afraid of hell themselves, and when under conviction they are afraid others will go there too. They seek happiness for themselves, and when self is not in the way they seek the same for others. Their great objective in praying is to secure the safety of those they pray for, just as their own safety is their one great objective in religion. They pity themselves and they pity others. If there were no danger, they would have no motive to pray either for themselves or for others.

20. *These professors of religion are very apt to be distressed by doubts.* And they are apt to talk a great deal about them. This makes up a great part of their life—the obsession with their doubts. Since they want only the enjoyment of a comfortable hope, as soon as they begin to doubt, it is all over for them, and so they make a great issue of it. They are not prepared to do anything for the church or for God, because they are always plagued and preoccupied with doubts.

21. *They are uneasy with the increasing calls for self-denial in order to do good.* These persons are annoyed by continual requests to give financially to missions, the poor, and to purchase Bibles, tracts, and the like. They are obliged to keep giving all the time in order to keep up their character and to maintain any hope, but they are very distressed about it.

22. *Not only is self-sacrificial giving distressful, it actually causes pain.* It is easy to see that if an individual has his heart set upon something, all the money he can save toward it is most encour-

aging to him. So if an individual finds it painful to give money for benevolent causes, it is clear that his heart is *not* set on those causes.

23. *This class of persons is not motivated to promote revivals.* It is safe to say revival is not among their religious objectives. If they participate in this work it is because they have been dragged into it. When a revival has gone on for a while and the excitement is great, they may come in and appear to be engaged in it. But you never see them taking the lead or striking out ahead of the rest, saying to the brethren, "Come on, let's do something for the Lord."

24. *They do not involve themselves in the conversion of sinners.* They may be instrumental for good in various ways (as so may Satan be). But as a general rule, they do not do the work of pulling sinners from the fire.

25. *They do not manifest distress when they see obvious sin.* They would never rebuke sin. In fact, they love to mingle in scenes where sin is committed. They want to be where vain conversation is indulged in and even join in with it. They enjoy worldly company and worldly pursuits.

26. *They take very little interest in published accounts of revivals, missions, or prayer.* If the work of missions is tried severely, they neither know about it nor care. If mission work prospers, they are unaware of it, much less have any interest in it. Very likely they do not read anything of a Christian nature.

27. *They do not aim at anything higher than a legalistic, negative religion.* The love of Christ does not constrain them to engage in warfare against sin or to see what good is in their power to do. What they do is done only because they think they must do it. Their spirituality is formal at best, heartless, and therefore worthless.

28. *They come reluctantly into all the special efforts of the church to worship or to promote good.* If a protracted meeting is proposed, you will generally find this class of persons hanging back and making objections or raising difficulties as long as they can.

29. *They do not enjoy private prayer*. They do not pray in private because they love to pray but because they think it is their duty and they dare not neglect it.

30. *They do not enjoy Bible reading or study*. They do not read the Bible because it is sweet to their souls. They read it because it is their duty to read it, and it would not do to profess to be a Christian and not read the Bible. Actual study is out of the question. In fact, they find it a dry book.

31. *They do not enjoy public prayer meetings*. The slightest excuse will keep them away. They never go unless they find it necessary for the sake of keeping up appearances or to maintain their fragile hope. And when they do go, instead of feeling their souls melted in love and fired with devotion, they become colder, listless, dull, and glad when it's over.

32. *They are hard put to understand what is meant by disinterested service*. To serve God because they love Him and not for the sake of reward is something they cannot comprehend.

33. *Their thoughts are not anxiously fixed upon the question, "When shall the world be converted to God?"* They do not agonize over such thoughts as, "O how long shall wickedness prevail?" or "When shall this wretched world be done with sin and death?" or "When shall men cease to sin against God?" They think more of the question, "When shall I die and go to heaven and be done with all my trials and cares?"

Remarks

1. I believe you will not think me extravagant when I say that the religion I have described appears to be that of a very large number in the church. To say the least, it is feared that a majority of professing Christians are of this description. And to say this is neither uncharitable nor censorious.

2. This religion is radically defective. There is nothing of true Christianity in it. It differs from Christianity as much as the Pharisees differed from Christ—as much as gospel religion differs from legalistic religion.

Now, let me ask you, to which of these classes do you belong? Or are you in neither? It may be that because you are sure you do not belong to the second class, you think you belong to the first; but when I come to describe the third class of professors, you may find your true character.

12

Religion of Public Opinion

"For they loved praise from men more than praise from God."

John 12:43

These words were spoken of certain individuals who refused to confess that Jesus was the Christ because He was extremely unpopular with the scribes and Pharisees and principal people of Jerusalem.

In my last lecture, I described a class of professors of religion who are moved to perform religious exercises out of hope and fear. They are sometimes moved by self-love and sometimes by selfishness. Their supreme objective is not to glorify God but to secure their own salvation.

Here I will point out the characteristics of a third class of professing Christians: those who love the praise of men more than the praise of God.

I don't want to be understood to imply that a mere regard for reputation has led this class to profess religion. Religion has always been too unpopular with the great majority to render it a general thing to become a professing Christian for reputation alone. But I mean that where it is not generally unpopular to become a professor of religion, and will not diminish one's popularity but rather increase it, a complex motive operates—the hope of securing happiness in a future world as well as an increased reputation here. And thus many are led to profess religion when, upon close examination, it is seen that the good opinion of their fellowmen is to be gained.

1. *They do what the apostle Paul says certain persons did in his day, and for that reason they remained ignorant of the true doctrine: They "measure themselves by themselves, and compare themselves among themselves."* There are many individuals who instead of making Jesus Christ their standard of comparison and the Bible their rule of life, obviously aim at neither. Their objective is to maintain a *respectable* profession of religion. Instead of seriously inquiring for themselves what the Bible teaches, and asking how Jesus Christ would act in a given situation, they look simply at the common run of professing Christians and are satisfied with doing what is commendable in their estimation. They prove by demonstration that their objective is not so much to do what the Bible teaches that professing Christians should do, but rather to do what is respectable in their view.

2. *This class of persons is not interested in elevating the standard of holiness in the church.* They are not troubled by the fact that the general standard is so low that it is a hindrance to bringing sinners to repentance. They think the present standard is high enough.

3. *They make a distinction between those requirements of God that are strongly enforced by public sentiment and those that are not.* All the sins that are frowned upon by public opinion, they will abstain from, but they do other things equally as sinful without a thought, because there is no condemnation of it among their peers. They fulfill every responsibility enforced by society around them, but shun those that are less enforced. They would not think

of staying away from public worship on the Sabbath, because if they did, they could not maintain their Christian reputation.

4. *This class of professors is apt to indulge in sins when they are away from their community that they would not commit while at home.* Many a man who is temperate at home, when he gets away will indulge himself, showing that he only refrains to save face and to represent some semblance of a Christian.

5. *Another development of the character of these individuals is that they indulge in secret sins.* If one allows oneself to sin secretly when he can get away with it, having no one to witness it, he should know that God sees it, nonetheless. He is more afraid of disgrace in the eye of mortals than of disgrace in the eye of God.

6. *These also indulge in secret omissions of responsibility that they would not dare to have known to others.* They may not practice secret sins or indulge in secret vice, but they neglect those Christian duties that, if it were known, would be considered disreputable to their Christian character.

7. *The conscience of this class of persons seems to be formed by principles other than those of the gospel.* They seem to have a conscience about things that are commonly required and none at all in those things that are not required by public sentiment. Show them a "Thus saith the Lord," and make them see that their course is inconsistent with Christian perfection and contrary to the interests of the kingdom of Christ, and yet they will not alter their behavior. They make it obvious that they have no regard for the requirements of God but only those of man. In short, they love the praise of men more than the praise of God.

8. *This class of persons generally dreads the thought of being considered fanatical.* They are generally ignorant of the first principle of religion: that the world is on a wrong course, that public sentiment in general is against God, and that everyone who intends to serve God must first of all turn his back on public opinion.

9. *They are very intent on making friends on both sides.* They always take the middle road. They avoid the reputation of being

overly righteous on the one hand, and of being lax or irreligious on the other. They are "fashionable Christians." No matter what God requires, they are determined to be so prudent as not to bring on themselves the censures of the world, nor to offend the enemies of God. They obviously have a greater regard for men than for God. And if they are ever in a situation where they must do what displeases their friends and neighbors or offend God, they will offend God. If public sentiment clashes with the commands of God, they will yield to public sentiment.

10. *They will do more to gain the applause of men than the applause of God*. This is evident from the fact that they will yield obedience only to those requirements of God that are sustained by strong public opinion. And although they will not exercise self-denial to gain the applause of God, they will sacrifice greatly to receive the applause of men.

11. *They are more anxious to know what men think of them than to know what God thinks of them*. If one of this class is a minister and preaches a sermon, he is more anxious to know what the people think of his message than to know what God thinks of it. And if he does anything that could be called a failure, the disgrace of it with men hurts him ten times more than the thought that he has dishonored God or hindered the salvation of souls. The women especially are more anxious about their appearance in the eyes of the world than in the eyes of God. They will go into the house of God with their hearts dark as midnight, while everything about their external appearance is attractive and pleasing.

12. *They refuse to confess their sins in the manner that the law of God requires, lest they should lose their reputation among men*. If they are ever required to make confession of more than they think consistent with their reputation, they are more anxious as to how it will affect their character before men than to know whether God is satisfied with them.

13. *They will yield to custom—what suits the welfare of mankind—even when they know it to be injurious to the cause of reli-*

gion. It is all about appearances and good graces before their fellowmen, and very little about what pleases God or fulfills the requirements of His law.

14. *They will do things of doubtful character*, even things the lawfulness of which is strongly in question—again, in obedience to public sentiment rather than in obedience to God.

15. *They are often so ashamed to speak for God that they simply refuse to do it*. Now, when a person is ashamed to do what God requires, it is plain that his own reputation is his idol. How many do you know who are ashamed to acknowledge Jesus Christ, ashamed to reprove sin in high places or low places, and ashamed to speak out when Christianity is assailed? If they supremely regarded God, could they ever be ashamed to speak of Him and defend Him? Suppose a man's wife was gossiped about. Would he be ashamed to defend her? By no means! If his children were mistreated, would he be ashamed to take their side? Not if he loved them. Shame could not deter him from defending his wife or his children. If a man was friendly to the administration of the government of his country, and heard it ill spoken of, would he be ashamed to defend it? He might not think it expedient to speak for other reasons, but if he were a true friend to the government, he would not be ashamed to speak on its behalf anywhere.

16. *They are opposed to all infringements on their time and resources*. They are disturbed by every new proposal in the church that draws upon their finances or encroaches on their personal time. Only when a significant number in the community creates a strong public sentiment in its favor will they adopt a new proposal, and not before.

17. *They are always distressed at what they call the "extremes" of the day*. They are afraid any reformation will destroy the church as they know it. They say we are carrying things too far, and we shall produce a public reaction. One instance that is cited is the Temperance Reformation. The real issue here is self-denial. Wherever that is called for, persons who are Christians in appearance only will revolt.

18. *They are often opposed to methods while they are unpopular and subject to reproach, but when they become popular, they go along with them.* This class of persons will go with the tide one way when a man is reproached and flow with the tide the other way when the same man is honored. There is only one exception. And that is when they have become so far committed to the opposition that they cannot come around to the other side without disgrace. Then they will be silent.

It has been this way with regard to the cause of missions, to a degree. If anything should turn up unfavorable to missions, so as to break the present power of public sentiment in its favor, you would find plenty of these fair-weather supporters turning to the opposition.

19. *If any measure is proposed to promote religion, they are very sensitive and scrupulous so as not to have anything done that is unpopular.* If they live in a large city, for instance, they will ask what the other churches think of such a measure. And if it is likely to bring reproach upon their church or their minister in view of the ungodly or of the other churches, they are distressed about it. No matter how much good it will do or how many souls it will save, they do not want to have anything done that would injure the respectability of their church.

20. *This class of persons never aims at promoting public bias in favor of godliness.* Contrarily, the true friends of God and man are always looking to change public bias in favor of righteousness and on challenging it when it is in error. The other class is ready to brand as imprudent or rash any man or anything that stems the tide of public opinion to turn it the other way.

Remarks

1. It is easy for persons to take credit for their sins—that is, to believe certain things are acts of spirituality when, in fact, they are only acts of hypocrisy. Unless you aim to live in full obedience to God in *everything*, the spirituality for which you claim credit is, in fact, sinning against God.

2. There is a great deal more apparent spirituality in the church than true spirituality.

3. There are many things that sinners suppose are good but which are abominable in the sight of God.

4. But for the love of reputation and the fear of disgrace, how many are there in the church who would live in open apostasy? How many do you know who would practice some vice were it not for the restraint of public sentiment, the fear of disgrace, and the desire to gain credit for supposed virtue? Only where a person is virtuous in obedience to God—whether the public favors it or not—is it true virtue.

I would like to know how many will determine to follow all the will of God—without regard to public opinion. Who will agree to take the Bible as your guide, Jesus Christ as your model, and do what is *right* in all cases, whatever men may say or think? Everyone who is not willing to take this stand must regard himself as a stranger to the grace of God. He is by no means justified. If he is not resolved to do what he knows to be right regardless of what the world thinks, he proves that he loves the praise of men more than the praise of God.

Epilogue

This has been a brief account of the life and preaching of Charles Grandison Finney—a lad who grew up in the backwoods of America without any knowledge of the gospel, a young lawyer who met the Lord Jesus in true penitence and prayer, a man devoted to the Scriptures and to the Savior, a revivalist whose tireless labors shook America and Britain in decades dark with human greed and godlessness. He was a pastor and college president whose ministry led multitudes to the Master and sent them to the ends of the earth in His glad service, a servant of Christ who still lives in Christian hearts the world over through the messages found in his books of sermons and his memoirs.

And Finney lives on in the hearts of those who need revival, in those who cry out for it. Pray for revival, and learn from Charles Finney its secrets.

Sources and Recommended Reading

Materials on the message and ministry of Charles Finney are few. Some are out of print but may still be found in libraries. The most outstanding are five works:

Finney, Charles G. *The Autobiography of Rev. Charles G. Finney*. New York: Revell, 1876. A revised version, condensed and edited by Helen Wessel, *The Autobiography of Charles G. Finney*, was published by Bethany House in 1977, and is still in print.

———. *Finney's Systematic Theology*, originally published in 1878. A complete and newly expanded edition was published by Bethany House in 1994, and is still in print.

———. *Lectures on Revivals of Religion*. New York: Revell, 1868. Out of print (o.p.).

———. *Lectures to Professing Christians*. New York: Revell, 1878. This was republished by Whitaker House in 1986, under the title *Crystal Christianity: A Vital Guide to Personal Revival*. o.p.

———. *Revival Lectures*. New York: Revell, 1868. o.p.

Other material on revival suggested for your reading includes:
Beardsley, Frank Grenville. *A History of American Revivals*. Boston: American Tract Society, 1904.

————. *A Mighty Winner of Souls, Charles G. Finney; A Study in Evangelism*. New York: American Tract Society, 1937.

Bonar, Andrew A., ed. *Memoirs of McCheyne, Including His Letters and Messages*. With a Biographical Introduction by S. Maxwell Coder. Chicago: Moody Press, 1947.

Chapman, J. Wilbur. *Revivals and Missions*. New York: Lentilhon & Co., 1900.

Edwards, Jonathan. *Thoughts on the Revival of Religion in New England, 1740*. To which is prefixed a narrative of the surprising work of God in Northampton, Mass., 1735. New York: American Tract Society, 1830.

Finney, Charles Grandison. *Sermons on Gospel Themes*. Oberlin: Goodrich, 1876.

Fish, Henry C. *Handbook of Revivals: For the Use of Winners of Souls*. Boston: Earle, 1874.

Keller, Charles Roy. *The Second Great Awakening in Connecticut*. New Haven: Yale University Press, 1942.

McCheyne, Robert Murray. *Revival Truth* (sermons previously unpublished, edited with a prefatory epistle to anxious inquirers on the work of the Lord Jesus Christ, and an introduction on the baptism of the Holy Ghost, especially addressed to believers who are praying for a great revival of vital religion, by William Reid). London: Nisbit, 1859.

Mode, Peter G. *Source Book and Bibliographical Guide for American Church History*. Kenosha, Wis.: George Banta Publishing Co., 1921.

Newell, William Wells. *Revivals: How and When?* New York: Armstrong, 1882.

Orr, J. Edwin. *The Second Evangelical Awakening in Britain*. London: Marshall, Morgan & Scott, Ltd., 1949.

Sprague, William B. *Lectures on Revivals of Religion*, 2nd ed. New York: Daniel Appleton & Co., 1833.

Sweet, William Warren. *Revivalism in America: Its Origin, Growth and Decline*. New York: Charles Scribner's Sons, 1944.

Thompson, Charles Lemuel. *Times of Refreshing, A History of*

American Revivals from 1740 to 1877, With Their Philosophy and Methods. Chicago: Smith, 1877.

Tracy, Joseph. *The Great Awakening: A History of the Revival of Religion in the Time of Edwards and Whitefield*. Boston: Tappan, 1842.

Tyler, Bennett. *Memoir of the Life and Character of Rev. Asahel Nettleton, D.D.*, 3rd ed. Boston: Doctrinal Tract and Book Society, 1850.

Tyler, W. S. *Prayer for Colleges: a Premium Essay*. New York: M. W. Dodd, 1855.

Wright, George Frederick. *Charles Grandison Finney*. New York: Houghton, 1891.